The Post-Millennial Return:

Why the Messiah Returns at the Millennium's End, *and* What It Means

V1.1, 6010 (2010)

By Norman B. Willis

By Norman B. Willis
Copyright © Nazarene Israel, 6010 (2010)
Good use permitted.
First Edition (v1.0) 6010 (2010 CE)

Nazarene Israel
P.O. Box 787
Anderson, CA 96007
USA

Email: servant@nazareneisrael.org.

May YHWH's name be glorified in all the earth.

In Yeshua's name,

Amein.

ABOUT THE ISLAMIC BEAST:

In the Second Edition of The Post-Millennial Return I hope to include new information about how Islam is the Fourth Beast of Daniel, and one of the beasts of the Revelation. I also hope to show how the Catholic Church and Islam are related in prophecy.

We know that Satan can manifest himself in many ways, and we know that he is active both in Islam, and in the Church system. Until I have time to write the Second Edition of this book I will try to post all of my studies on the website.

Shalom,

Norman

Table of Contents:

Preface	7
What is a 'Pre-Millennial' Return?	9
Understanding Revelation 20:4-6	13
Eleven More Witnesses	32
The Post-Millennial Model	53
About Spiritual Resurrections	56
The Second Resurrection	71
The First Resurrection	81
The Two Sticks	89
The Millennial Land	103
New Heavens, New Earth	130
Zechariah 12-14 Explained	151
The Mark of the Beast	174
America: Daughter of Babylon	206
The Abomination of Desolation	246
Building the Stick	274

Author's Notes:

Shalom, Nazarene.

People often ask what version of Scripture I use. Unless otherwise noted, I have generally begun with the New King James, and then corrected for the set-apart names. I have also corrected any wording that does not accurately impart the meaning of the original Hebrew and/or Aramaic.

With the exception of its desecration the names, the New King James Version is generally accurate, and it captures the essence of the original languages in some ninety-nine percent of all cases. However, by their very nature, study guides like this one spend a lot of time focusing on errors that need to be corrected (whether they are errors in translation or errors in doctrine).

When pointing out translational errors, I have tried to display the original Hebrew and/or Aramaic alongside the English, so that the reader can have the original source languages present. The Hebrew comes from the Hebrew Masoretic Text which, while amended, is the text most commonly used by our brothers in Judah.

For the Aramaic, unless otherwise noted I have used the Hebrew translation of the corrected version of the Jerusalem Bible Society (JBS) Peshitta Aramaic (2005 CE). My reason for using the Hebrew was that many readers find the Aramaic Estrangelo script to be unfamiliar and daunting, and the points were made just as well by using the JBS Hebrew translation.

Finally, while I am often asked to provide Western-style footnotes (and other Western-style cross-references), I have typically avoided this practice, as my belief is that Scripture is the highest and best authority on all matters of doctrine. If one cannot understand a point simply by looking at the relevant passage of Scripture, then why would it make sense to reference another mortal author? Is anyone's word more important than Elohim's (G-d's)?

In the past, both Ephraimites and Jews have paid more attention to the words of man than they have to the Word of Elohim. My approach, therefore, is simply to show what YHWH's Word states, and then provide only enough commentary to show how the verses relate to each other. My hope in this is to lead people to focus on His Word (and not my own). My commentary is valuable only insofar as it explains what the Scriptures actually say.

Future editions of this work will incorporate additional information about Islam as one fulfillment of the Beast of the Revelation. If you have questions, suggestions or comments about this publication, please let me know of this error, so we can correct it in the next edition.

I ask that you please pray to the Father, and ask Him to cause you to prove all things, and hold fast only to that which is good.

Shalom,

Norman B. Willis
In the Dispersion
2007 CE (+/- 6007 HRT)

Preface

Do you want to take part in the restoration of the original apostolic faith? You can. It is going on right now.

Do you want to help the Jewish people to accept (and love) their Messiah? This book can show you how to be a part of that.

This book assumes a working knowledge of the information presented in *Nazarene Israel: The Original Faith of the Apostles*, third edition or later. You can obtain your copy of this book at cost through the Nazarene Israel website, **www.nazareneisrael.org**, or through **www.Amazon.com**.

There are many myths and misconceptions about the end times. If you want to know what Scripture really speaks of for the end times, read on....

Kepha Bet (2nd Peter) 3:10-13

10 But the Day of YHWH will come as a thief in the night, in which the heavens will pass away with a great noise, and the elements will melt with fervent heat; both the earth and the works that are in it will be burned up.
11 Therefore, since all these things will be dissolved, what manner of persons ought you to be in set-apart conduct and set-apartness,
12 looking for and hastening the coming of the day of Elohim, because of which the heavens will be dissolved, being on fire, and the elements will melt with fervent heat?
13 Nevertheless we, according to His promise, look for new heavens and a new earth in which righteousness dwells.

What is a 'Pre-Millennial' Return?

Most scholars regard the Book of Genesis as being prophetic, in that events recorded in Genesis establish patterns that show up again later in Scripture. The Book of Genesis, then, tells us that when Elohim (G-d) was creating the earth, He worked for six days, and then rested on the seventh day. Elohim 'sanctified' the seventh day, or 'set it apart' from all of the others (as being special).

> *B'reisheet (Genesis) 2:1-3*
> *1 Thus the heavens and the earth, and all the host of them, were finished.*
> *2 And on the seventh day Elohim ended His work which He had done, and He rested on the seventh day from all His work which He had done.*
> *3 Then Elohim blessed the seventh day and sanctified, because in it He rested from all His work which Elohim had created and made.*

The Apostle Kepha (Peter) then tells us not to forget that in prophecy, one day can sometimes represent a thousand earth years.

> *Kepha Bet (2nd Peter) 3:8-9*
> *8 But, beloved, do not forget this one thing: That with YHWH one day is as a thousand years, and a thousand years is as one day.*

Many scholars tell us that if a day in prophecy can sometimes represent a thousand earth years, and if the Creation Week was seven days long, then this means that the earth is supposed to exist for seven thousand years (after which it will be destroyed). Some of these scholars further tell us that since YHWH worked for six of these days and then rested on the seventh, this means that mankind will labor for six thousand years, and then the seventh thousand years will be special, in that it will somehow be more restful.

Scholars often call this final thousand years of earth's history the 'Sabbath Millennium.' They also sometimes call it the 'Millennial Reign of the Messiah,' in that they assume the Messiah will return back to earth in physical form at the start of this final thousand years. This theory is sometimes called Pre-Millennial Return Theory, and it is based in large part on a particular reading of Revelation 20:4-6, which tells us that the saints will rule and reign 'with' the Messiah for a thousand years.

> *Gilyana (Revelation) 20:4-6*
> *4 And I saw thrones, and they sat on them, and judgment was committed to them. Then I saw the souls of those who had been beheaded for their witness to Yeshua and for the word of Elohim (G-d), who had not worshiped the beast or his image, and had not received his mark on their foreheads or on their hands. And they lived and reigned with Messiah for a thousand years.*
> *5 But the rest of the dead did not live again until the thousand years were finished. This is the first resurrection.*

> *6 Blessed and set-apart is he who has part in the first resurrection. Over such the second death has no power, but they shall be priests of Elohim and of Messiah, and shall reign with Him a thousand years.*

Because verses 4 and 6 tell us that the believers will reign 'with' the Messiah for a thousand years, Pre-Millennial Return Theory tells us that the Messiah must return back to earth in physical form a thousand years before the earth ends. Otherwise, they ask, how could the believers rule 'with' Him for a thousand years?

It might seem like Revelation 20:4-6 is conclusive, but as we study the matter out, we find there are actually many reasons why the Messiah cannot return to earth in physical form a thousand years before the earth's end. One relatively simple reason is how the Apostle Kepha (Peter) tells us that when the Messiah returns, the heavens will pass away with a great noise, and the earth (and everything in it) will be burned up. [Kepha here refers to Yeshua's return as the Day of YHWH (the 'Day of the L-rd').]

> *Kepha Bet (2nd Peter) 3:10-13*
> *10 But the Day of YHWH will come as a thief in the night, in which the heavens will pass away with a great noise, and the elements will melt with fervent heat; both the earth and the works that are in it will be burned up.*
> *11 Therefore, since all these things will be dissolved, what manner of persons ought you to be in set-apart conduct and set-apartness,*

12 looking for and hastening the coming of the day of Elohim, because of which the heavens will be dissolved, being on fire, and the elements will melt with fervent heat?
13 Nevertheless we, according to His promise, look for new heavens and a new earth in which righteousness dwells.

This passage indicates that when Yeshua returns, the heavens will pass away with a great noise, the elements will melt with a fervent heat, and both the earth and everything in it will be burned up. In that day, the heavens will also be dissolved (being on fire).

However, how can Yeshua rule 'with' the saints for a thousand years, if the earth (and everything in it) is to be destroyed upon His arrival?

Understanding Revelation 20:4-6

Protestant Christianity teaches us that the Messiah Yeshua (or 'Jesus') will return to earth at the start of a thousand year period of time popularly known as, *'The Millennium.'* According to this doctrine of a *'Pre-Millennial'* Return, the Messiah Yeshua was supposed to return to earth in or around the year 2000, to rule and reign over the earth for a thousand years.

There are many different versions of Pre-Millennial Return Theory. A few of the more popular versions of this theory are called:

- The Rapture
- The Place of Safety
- A Place in the Wilderness; and
- Heaven for Seven Years

While all of these different versions have some slight differences with each other, most of them share certain fundamental core beliefs. Among these core beliefs are the ideas that the Messiah will:

- Come in the clouds (Acts 1:9-11);
- At the start of the Millennium (Rev. 20:4-6);
- Circle the earth (Revelation 1:7);
- Catch the saints up to be with Him in a kind of a 'Rapture' or 'Catching Away' (1st Thess. 4:17);
- Land on the Mount of Olives (Zechariah 14);
- Smite the enemies of Israel (Revelation 20:9);
- Build Ezekiel's Temple (Zechariah 3:8);

- Serve in this temple both as Israel's King, and as Israel's High Priest (Zechariah 6, Hebrews 6:20).
- Finally, the saints will be given supernatural bodies, which will sustain them for a thousand years while they rule and reign sitting right next to Yeshua (Revelation 20:4-6).

It is clear that Pre-Millennial Return Theory is based on certain passages of Scripture; however, this book will show how Pre-Millennial Return Theory takes these passages out of context, and thus leads its adherents to the wrong conclusions.

For example, Pre-Millennial Return Theory teaches that the Book of the Revelation is a simple, straight-forward chronicle of events that will take place in the end times. However, Revelation is not such a straight-forward chronicle of events. Rather, it is a *vision* that speaks in highly symbolic language.

> **Gilyana (Revelation) 1:10**
> **10 I was in the Spirit on the Day of YHWH, and I heard behind me a loud voice, as of a trumpet....**

The expression "in the Spirit" is used in prophecy to alert the reader that he is reading pure symbolism, and that he should be careful not to take what he is reading literally. Since the very first chapter of Revelation tells us that it is speaking in purely symbolic language, then it makes no real sense to assume that we are reading about literal events that will play out on earth just exactly as they are depicted in the vision.

Four chapters later, Revelation 4:1-2 tells us that we are still "in the Spirit," and that we are still reading about a vision that takes place "in heaven" (and not on earth). Thus, Revelation is speaking about symbolic events that will look much different when they play out on earth, than they appeared in the vision.

> *Gilyana (Revelation) 4:1-2*
> *4:1 After these things I looked, and behold, a door standing open in heaven. And the first voice which I heard was like a trumpet speaking with me, saying, "Come up here, and I will show you things which must take place after this."*
> *2 Immediately I was in the Spirit; and behold, a throne set in heaven, and One sat on the throne.*

Visions rarely play out on earth just exactly as things are depicted in the vision. That is not to say that visions do not foretell actual events, because they do. However, consider the vision of the great statue that King Nebuchadnezzar dreamed of in Daniel Chapter Two. When the event played out on earth, did the earthly events look like what the vision depicted?

> *Daniel 2:31-35*
> *31 "You, O king, were watching; and behold, a great image! This great image, whose splendor was excellent, stood before you; and its form was awesome.*
> *32 This image's head was of fine gold, its chest and arms of silver, its belly and thighs of bronze,*

33 its legs of iron, its feet partly of iron and partly of clay.
34 You watched while a stone was cut out without hands, which struck the image on its feet of iron and clay, and broke them in pieces.
35 Then the iron, the clay, the bronze, the silver, and the gold were crushed together, and became like chaff from the summer threshing floors; the wind carried them away so that no trace of them was found. And the stone that struck the image became a great mountain and filled the whole earth.

This vision was not given to warn Nebuchadnezzar of a real stone that would fly out of a real mountain, and smash a real statue on earth. Rather, it was a highly symbolic vision that foretold the succession of the Babylonian, Medo-Persian, Greek, Roman and then Islamic Empires, as well as how they would ultimately be broken by Yeshua, who is here symbolized as a "stone that was cut out of the mountain without hands."

Was Yeshua literally part of a stone mountain? And was He literally cut out of a mountain (without hands)? The thought is absurd; but that is what one would effectively have to believe, if one was to believe that visions must always be fulfilled exactly as they are depicted.

So if prophecies do not have to be fulfilled literally in order to be fulfilled completely, then why do the pre-millennial return theorists tell us that the Book of the Revelation will be fulfilled literally, when Revelation itself tells us that it is a spiritual vision?

Why indeed? By the time we reach Revelation Chapter Seventeen, we are told that we are still "in the Spirit;" and then the text even comes right out and tells us that the things we read about are symbolic of *other things*.

> *Gilyana (Revelation) 17:3-18*
> *3 So he carried me away in the Spirit into the wilderness. And I saw a woman sitting on a scarlet beast which was full of names of blasphemy, having seven heads and ten horns.*
> *4 The woman was arrayed in purple and scarlet, and adorned with gold and precious stones and pearls, having in her hand a golden cup full of abominations and the filthiness of her fornication.*
> *5 And on her forehead a name was written: MYSTERY, BABYLON THE GREAT, THE MOTHER OF HARLOTS AND OF THE ABOMINATIONS OF THE EARTH.*
> *6 I saw the woman, drunk with the blood of the saints and with the blood of the martyrs of Yeshua. And when I saw her, I marveled with great amazement.*

Notice the messenger (angel) tells us the meanings *behind* the symbolism we have just been shown.

> *7 But the messenger said to me, "Why did you marvel? I will tell you the mystery of the woman and of the beast that carries her, which has the seven heads and the ten horns.*

> *8 The beast that you saw was, and is not, and will ascend out of the bottomless pit and go to perdition. And those who dwell on the earth will marvel, whose names are not written in the Book of Life from the foundation of the world, when they see the beast that was, and is not, and yet is.*
> *9 "Here is the mind which has wisdom: The seven heads are seven mountains on which the woman sits.*

Verse nine tells us that "the seven heads are the seven mountains upon which the woman sits." In other words, the seven heads are symbolic of the Seven Hills of Rome, and the Beast is symbolic of the replacement-theology Church system (i.e., the Roman Catholic Church and her daughters, the Protestant Churches.)

> *10 There are also seven kings. Five have fallen, one is, and the other has not yet come. And when he comes, he must continue a short time.*
> *11 The beast that was, and is not, is himself also the eighth, and is of the seven, and is going to perdition.*

Next we are told that the ten 'horns' are symbolic of ten Roman-style economic-imperialist kingships (the latest of which, many scholars feel, is a United Europe).

> *12 "The ten horns which you saw are ten kings who have received no kingdom as yet, but they receive authority for one hour as kings with the beast.*

> *13 These are of one mind, and they will give their power and authority to the beast.*
> *14 These will make war with the Lamb, and the Lamb will overcome them, for He is Master of Masters and King of kings; and those who are with Him are called, chosen, and faithful."*

So symbolic is the language contained in Revelation that water does not even represent water!

> *15 Then he said to me, "The waters which you saw, where the harlot sits, are peoples, multitudes, nations, and tongues.*
> *16 And the ten horns which you saw on the beast, these will hate the harlot, make her desolate and naked, eat her flesh and burn her with fire.*
> *17 For Elohim has put it into their hearts to fulfill His purpose, to be of one mind, and to give their kingdom to the beast, until the words of Elohim are fulfilled.*
> *18 And the woman whom you saw is that great city which reigns over the kings of the earth."*

The 'woman' is a city, the 'waters' are peoples, the ten 'horns' are ten kingdoms, and nothing will ever play out on earth just as it is seen in the vision, because it is not supposed to. The phrase "in the Spirit" appears *only* in Revelation and in the 'Dry Bones' prophecy in Ezekiel 37, and in both places it alerts us to the fact that we are reading a highly symbolic vision.

By the time we get to Revelation 20:1-3, we should be able to see that we are *still* reading about purely symbolic events, because the language describes things that do not exist here on earth.

> **Gilyana (Revelation) 20:1-3**
> **20:1 Then I saw a messenger (angel) coming down from heaven, having the key to the bottomless pit and a great chain in his hand.**
> **2 He laid hold of the dragon, that serpent of old, who is the Devil and Satan, and bound him for a thousand years;**
> **3 and he cast him into the bottomless pit, and shut him up, and set a seal on him, so that he should deceive the nations no more till the thousand years were finished. But after these things he must be released for a little while.**

Verse one tells us about a messenger that comes down from heaven, "having the key to the bottomless pit" in his hand. We should be able to recognize this as symbolic language, because there is no bottomless pit here on earth. When I have confronted pre-millennial theorists with the fact that there is no bottomless pit, I have been given all sorts of explanations, including the following:

1. While there is presently no bottomless pit, YHWH plans bend the space-time-continuum, in order to make one.
2. The 'bottomless pit' is actually the Marianas Trench (which is not bottomless).

3. The earth is hollow; and therefore what will happen is that the messenger (angel) will carry Satan up to the North Pole, because that is where the entrance to the molten-lava core of the hollow-earth is.

These are real stories. However, while YHWH can and does work wonders, is it good to resort to magical thinking when explaining prophecy?

We can see another proof of how Revelation speaks in symbolic language, in that Revelation 20:2 (above) tells us that Satan is a dragon. This stands in direct opposition to Isaiah 14:16, which tells us that Satan is a man.

> *Yeshayahu (Isaiah) 14:16-17*
> *16 "Those who see you will gaze at you, and consider you, saying: 'Is this the man who made the earth tremble, who shook kingdoms,*
> *17 Who made the world as a wilderness and destroyed its cities, who did not open the house of his prisoners?'"*

How do we reconcile Revelation 20:2, which tells us that Satan is a dragon, compared to Isaiah 14:16-17, which tells us that Satan a man? Or is Satan perhaps maybe a serpent, as is in the Garden of Eden?

> *B'reisheet (Genesis) 3:1-2*
> *1a Now the serpent was more cunning than any beast of the field which YHWH Elohim had made.*

> **1b And he said to the woman, "Has Elohim indeed said, 'You shall not eat of every tree of the garden'?"**

The truth is that Satan can be anything YHWH wants him to be, so that Israel can have a whetstone to be sharpened against. Satan can be a man, a dragon, a serpent, a perfect covering cherub (Ezekiel 28:14-15), or whatever other thing that YHWH wants him to be at the moment. The language of Revelation 20:2 just so happens to portray Satan as a dragon, which works fine because the entire Book of the Revelation is a highly symbolic vision that depicts events that take place in the heavenly realms.

In contrast to this, Pre-Millennial Return Theory tells us that Revelation 20 speaks of events as they take place here on earth, because it tends to support their theory that the Messiah will return back to earth in physical form a thousand years before the earth's end.

> *Gilyana (Revelation) 20:4-6*
> *4 And I saw thrones, and they sat on them, and judgment was committed to them. Then I saw the souls of those who had been beheaded for their witness to Yeshua and for the word of Elohim (G-d), who had not worshiped the beast or his image, and had not received his mark on their foreheads or on their hands. And they lived and reigned with Messiah for a thousand years.*
> *5 But the rest of the dead did not live again until the thousand years were finished. This is the first resurrection.*

6 Blessed and set-apart is he who has part in the first resurrection. Over such the second death has no power, but they shall be priests of Elohim and of Messiah, and shall reign with Him a thousand years.

Why do the pre-millennialists tell us that verses 4-6 depict literal events as they take place here on earth, when none of the rest of the Book of the Revelation depicts literal events here on earth? Isn't it taking these verses out of context, to insist that they be taken literally, when none of the rest of the Book of the Revelation is to be taken literally?

How reasonable is it that an entire book of prophecy depicts events as they take place in the heavenly realms, except for three lone verses, which are supposed to be taken literally?

When I have asked pre-millennialists I know why we should take three lone verses out of their greater overall context, and assume they are literal when the surrounding passage is symbolic, they have typically responded by rhetorically asking how the saints can reign 'with' Yeshua for a thousand years, if Yeshua will not be physically present during that time. The answer, of course, is that the Book of the Revelation is not the only place we are told that YHWH/Yeshua is "with" His people Israel. There are many places where Scripture tells us that YHWH either is already with, or has been with His people Israel, and in none of these cases was YHWH/Yeshua literally (physically) present.

For example, in Genesis 39:2-3, we read that YHWH was "with" Joseph (even while Joseph was in prison).

> B'reisheet (Genesis) 39:2-3
> 2 YHWH was with Joseph, and he was a successful man; and he was in the house of his master the Egyptian.
> 3 And his master saw that YHWH was with him, and that YHWH made all he did to prosper in his hand.

YHWH was also "with" the prophet Samuel.

> Shemu'el Aleph (1st Samuel) 3:19-20
> 19 So Samuel grew, and YHWH was with him and let none of his words fall to the ground.

First Samuel Eighteen tells us that YHWH was "with" David (even before he was anointed king).

> Shemu'el Aleph (1st Samuel) 18:12-14
> 12 Now (King) Shaul was afraid of David, because YHWH was with him, but he had departed from (King) Shaul.
> 13 Therefore Shaul removed him from his presence, and made him his captain over a thousand; and he went out and came in before the people.
> 14 And David behaved wisely in all his ways, and YHWH was with him.

YHWH was "with" Hezekiah.

> Melachim Bet (2nd Kings) 18:7
> 7 YHWH was with him; he prospered wherever he went.

If we need more examples, YHWH was "with" Pinchas, the son of Eleazar.

> **Divre HaYamim (1st Chronicles) 9:20**
> **20 And Pinchas the son of Eleazar had been the officer over them in time past; YHWH was with him.**

This phenomenon is not solely restricted to the Tanach (the 'Old' Covenant) either, for we read that the hand of YHWH would be "with" Yeshua.

> **Luqa (Luke) 1:66**
> **66 And all those who heard them kept them in their hearts, saying, "What kind of child will this be?" And the hand of YHWH was with him.**

Further, in the Great Commission, Yeshua tells us that He will be "with" us, even until the end of the world. [Let us note that the word 'world' in Hebrew would be עוֹלָם ('olam').]

> **Mattai (Matthew) 28:18-20**
> **18 And Yeshua came and spoke to them, saying, "All authority has been given to Me in heaven and on earth.**
> **19 Go therefore and make disciples of all the nations, baptizing them in the name of the Father, and of the Son, and of the Set-apart Spirit,**
> **20 teaching them to observe all things that I have commanded you; and lo, I am with you always, even to the end of the world (עוֹלָם)." Amein.**

Isaiah tells us that Elohim (G-d) is always "with" Israel:

> **Yeshayahu (Isaiah) 8:10**
> **10 Take counsel together, but it will come to nothing; speak the word, but it will not stand, for Elohim is with us."**

Indeed, in the previous chapter, in Isaiah 7:14 we are told that one of the Messiah's Names is 'Immanuel,' meaning, "Elohim *with* us."

> **Yeshayahu (Isaiah) 7:14**
> **14 Therefore YHWH Himself will give you a sign: behold, the virgin shall conceive and bear a Son, and shall call His name Immanuel (Elohim 'with' us).**

Scripture shows that YHWH has been "with" His people all along. For Him to be "with" His people is not new. To prove this, please consider a simple question:

Is YHWH with you?

So, if YHWH is "with" us even now (even though He may not be *physically* present), then what does Revelation 20:4-6 mean when it says that the saints will reign "with" Messiah for a thousand years?

> **Gilyana (Revelation) 20:4-6**
> **4 And I saw thrones, and they sat on them, and judgment was committed to them. Then I saw the souls of those who had been beheaded for their witness to Yeshua and for the word of Elohim (G-d), who had not worshiped**

> *the beast or his image, and had not received his mark on their foreheads or on their hands. And they lived and reigned with Messiah for a thousand years.*
> *5 But the rest of the dead did not live again until the thousand years were finished. This is the first resurrection.*
> *6 Blessed and set-apart is he who has part in the first resurrection. Over such the second death has no power, but they shall be priests of Elohim and of Messiah, and shall reign with Him a thousand years.*

YHWH sometimes inspires prophecy in riddles, to keep the meaning sealed up until the end times. Revelation 20:4-6 is one of those riddles. The emphasis is not that Israel will reign **with** Yeshua *physically present*, but that Israel will **reign** with Yeshua (because they have not reigned for thousands of years). That is, for the first time in thousands of years, all twelve tribes of Israel will reunite in the Land. And, for the first time ever, Israel will rule over the nations *in the Spirit of Yeshua,* because this time, Yeshua will be "with" them.

When Satan is bound in the Pit, all twelve tribes of Israel will be reunited, and together they will reign over the kingdoms of the earth in a way they have not reigned since the days of Kings David and Solomon. However, notice that Yeshua cannot be physically present during that time, because Scripture tells us that the saints will rule and reign *in Yeshua's stead*, with His rod of iron. This is seen by the interplay of Psalms 2:7-9, where Yeshua is given power over the nations, and Revelation 2:26-27, where Israel is given this power.

> *Tehillim (Psalms) 2:7-9*
> *7 "I will declare the decree: YHWH has said to Me, 'You are My Son, today I have begotten You.*
> *8 Ask of Me, and I will give You the nations for Your inheritance, and the ends of the earth for Your possession.*
> *9 You shall break them with a rod of iron; You shall dash them to pieces like a potter's vessel.'"*

In this Psalm, Yeshua tells us that His Father has given Him authority to rule over the nations with a rod of iron; and that He will dash them to pieces, like a potter's vessel. However, now let us look at Revelation 2:26-27, where Yeshua tells us that He plans to do this ruling and reigning vicariously (through us).

> *Gilyana (Revelation) 2:26-27*
> *26 And he who overcomes (Israel), and keeps My works until the end, to him I will give power over the nations —*
> *27 'He shall rule them with a rod of iron; they shall be dashed to pieces like the potter's vessels' — as I also have received from My Father....*

In Psalm 2:7-9 (above), Yeshua told us that YHWH the Father gave Him the authority to rule the nations with a rod of iron. Then in Revelation 2:27 (immediately above), Yeshua tells us that His people Israel will do this ruling for Him (in His stead). This is fits perfectly with how Revelation depicts Yeshua ruling over the nations, and yet when the vision plays out on earth, it is Yeshua's body (Israel) that is doing the ruling.

In this way, Yeshua will be 'with' His people Israel for a thousand years, as they rule over the nations, with His rod of iron.

The four verses following Revelation 20:4-6 are also written in symbolic language, and we can be fairly certain that these events will probably not play out on earth just exactly as they are depicted in the vision, because they speak of things that do not exist on earth.

> *Gilyana (Revelation) 20:7-10*
> *7 Now when the thousand years have expired, Satan will be released from his prison*
> *8 and will go out to deceive the nations which are in the four corners of the earth, Gog and Magog, to gather them together to battle, whose number is as the sand of the sea.*
> *9 They went up on the breadth of the earth and surrounded the camp of the saints and the beloved city. And fire came down from Elohim out of heaven and devoured them.*
> *10 The devil, who deceived them, was cast into the lake of fire and brimstone where the beast and the false prophet are. And they will be tormented day and night forever and ever.*

The events depicted here cannot be literal, because the Beast depicted here is not a literal beast, but is the Roman system. Also, there is no literal Lake of Fire and Brimstone here on earth. When I have asked my pre-millennialist friends where this alleged earthly Lake of Fire and Brimstone is, I have been told that:

1. The Sea of Galilee is so wet that it could easily spontaneously combust; and that
2. The Dead Sea has so much salt in it that it would probably catch on fire and burn forever, if a nuclear weapon were dropped on it.

[Note: Salt is non-combustible, and does not burn.]

Surely, the Devil, the Beast, the False Prophet and the Lake of Fire are symbolic of something that exists here on earth. However, the point is that they are *symbols*. We almost certainly cannot expect to see a literal Lake of Fire and Brimstone, or a literal Bottomless Pit, or a literal dragon. For this reason, we also should not insist that Yeshua will be physically present during the Millennium, when 2nd Peter 3:8 tells us that the earth will be destroyed when Yeshua returns.

Timoteos Bet (2nd Timothy) 3:16-17

16 All Scripture is given by inspiration of Elohim, and is profitable for doctrine, for reproof, for correction, for instruction in righteousness,

17 that the man of Elohim may be complete, thoroughly equipped for every good work.

Eleven More Witnesses

Pre-Millennial Return Theory is logically incompatible with numerous prophecies. For just one example, most versions of a pre-millennial return tell us that the saints will be brought back to the Land of Israel by supernatural means (i.e., in a cloud, or in a 'Rapture,' or a 'catching away' of some kind). This idea is contrary to the prophecy over the return of the Lost Ten Tribes given in Isaiah 66:20-21, which tells us that the tribes (i.e., the Christians) will return back to the Land of Israel by natural means (and not supernatural ones).

> *Yeshayahu (Isaiah) 66:20-21*
> *20 Then they shall bring all your brethren for an offering to YHWH out of all nations, on horses and in chariots and in litters, on mules and on camels, to My holy mountain Jerusalem," says YHWH, "as the children of Israel bring an offering in a clean vessel into the House of YHWH.*
> *21 And I will also take some of them for priests and Levites," says YHWH.*

One can well imagine that the horses, chariots, litters, mules and camels of this passage are the trains, planes, automobiles and buses of the modern era. However, what we need to see is that Isaiah does not speak of the Lost Ten Tribes returning to the Land of Israel by supernatural means, but by natural ones. It does not say they will return to the Land in a cloud.

The second witness that Pre-Millennial Return Theory is wrong is found in Jeremiah. Speaking also of the time of the return of the Lost Ten Tribes (at the beginning of the Millennium), Jeremiah 3:18 tells us:

> **Yirmeyahu (Jeremiah) 3:18**
> **18 "In those days the House of Judah shall walk with the House of Israel, and they shall come together out of the land of the north to the land that I have given as an inheritance to your fathers.**

This verse does not tell us that the Lost Ten Tribes will return back to the Land of Israel in a cloud; but that they will 'walk' back home to the Land. While Jeremiah may be speaking in symbolic language, he never speaks of a supernatural means of return (such as being caught up in a cloud). Rather, he only speaks of natural ones (such as walking).

Now we begin with the logical-dilemma proofs. These are all based on the fact that all Scripture is inspired, and is given by inspiration of Elohim.

In his second epistle to Timothy, the Apostle Shaul tells us that *all* Scripture is given by inspiration of Elohim:

> **Timoteos Bet (2nd Timothy) 3:16-17**
> **16 All Scripture is given by inspiration of Elohim, and is profitable for doctrine, for reproof, for correction, for instruction in righteousness,**
> **17 that the man of Elohim may be complete, thoroughly equipped for every good work.**

If *all* Scripture is given by inspiration of Elohim, and if *all* Scripture is profitable for doctrine, then whatever doctrines we have must agree with *all* of Scripture. However, Pre-Millennial Return Theory fails this test.

As we explain in the *Nazarene Israel* study, Yeshua told us not to think that He was sent to do away with even the smallest part of the Torah (the Law of Moses), or of the Prophets.

> *Mattai (Matthew) 5:17-18*
> *17 "Do not think that I came to destroy the Torah or the Prophets. I did not come to destroy but to fulfill.*
> *18 For assuredly, I say to you, till heaven and earth pass away, one jot or one tittle will by no means pass from the Torah till all is fulfilled.*

Since Yeshua said He did not come to destroy the Torah or the Prophets, the prophecies contained in the Torah and the Prophets must still be in effect (and must some day come to pass). However, as this chapter will show, if Pre-Millennial Return Theory is correct, and Yeshua returns at the start of the Millennium (and then goes on to rule and reign supreme for a thousand years), many of the inspired prophecies can never come to pass.

The problem is this: If Yeshua reigns *supreme* during the thousand years, then logically, no one else can reign during that same time frame (or by definition, Yeshua would not be reigning 'supreme'.) However, the inspired prophecies tell us that a number of other people (who are clearly not Yeshua) will be reigning during that same time frame.

What we end up with is a logical dilemma: either Yeshua cannot be physically reigning supreme (i.e., He cannot be physically present during the Millennium), or else the prophecies which tell us that *other* people will be reigning during the Millennium are wrong (which is a logical impossibility). Therefore, Pre-Millennial Return Theory loses, by default.

For example, Genesis 49:22-24 speaks of a great national leader who will arise from the Tribe of Joseph. This is an important passage, so let us look at it in the original Hebrew.

Genesis 49:22-24 22 "Joseph is a fruitful bough, a fruitful bough by a well: his branches run over the wall. 23 The archers have bitterly grieved him, shot at him and hated him. 24 But his bow remained in strength, and the arms of his hands were made strong by the hands of the Mighty One of Jacob. From there is the Shepherd, the Stone of Israel.	(22) בֵּן פֹּרָת יוֹסֵף בֵּן פֹּרָת עֲלֵי עָיִן ׀ בָּנוֹת צָעֲדָה עֲלֵי שׁוּר : (23) וַיְמָרֲרֻהוּ וָרֹבּוּ ׀ וַיִּשְׂטְמֻהוּ בַּעֲלֵי חִצִּים : (24) וַתֵּשֶׁב בְּאֵיתָן קַשְׁתּוֹ וַיָּפֹזּוּ זְרֹעֵי יָדָיו ׀ מִידֵי אֲבִיר יַעֲקֹב מִשָּׁם רֹעֶה אֶבֶן יִשְׂרָאֵל

Verse 24 tells us that there would be a man called 'the Shepherd,' and 'The Stone of Israel.' However, this man would not arise from the Tribe of Judah (as Yeshua did), but from the Tribe of *Joseph*:

24b From there (Joseph) is the Shepherd, the Stone of Israel.	מִשָּׁם רֹעֶה אֶבֶן יִשְׂרָאֵל

It might at first seem baffling that any shepherd would ever arise from the Tribe of Joseph. After all, Yeshua tells us that *He* is the Good Shepherd.

> *Yochanan (John) 10:11*
> *11 "I am the good shepherd. The good shepherd gives His life for the sheep."*

Yeshua, however, did not arise from the Tribe of Joseph, but from the Tribe of Judah.

> *Ivrim (Hebrews) 7:14*
> *14 For it is evident that our Master arose from (the Tribe of) Judah....*

Further, how can Genesis 49:24 speak of the 'Stone of Israel' coming from Joseph? Isaiah tells us Yeshua is the Stone of Stumbling, and the Rock of Offense.

> *Yeshayahu (Isaiah) 8:14-15*
> *14 He will be as a sanctuary, but a stone of stumbling and a rock of offense to both the houses of Israel, (and) as a trap and a snare to the inhabitants of Jerusalem.*
> *15 And many among them shall stumble; they shall fall and be broken, be snared and taken."*

However, once again we are left with the logical contradiction that while Yeshua was from the Tribe of Judah, Genesis 49:24 speaks of a 'Stone of Israel' that comes from the Tribe of Joseph.

No one can born into both the Tribe of Joseph, *and* the Tribe of Judah (not even Yeshua); and as we will see, this also gives us yet one more witness as to why Yeshua cannot possibly come back to earth at the start of the Millennium.

In Isaiah 42:8, YHWH tells us that He will not share His glory with any human being.

> ***Yeshayahu (Isaiah) 42:8***
> ***8 I am YHWH, that is My Name; and My glory I will not give to another, nor My praise to carved images.***

In addition to this, Yeshua tells us that He and His Father are one.

> ***Yochanan (John) 10:30***
> ***30 I and My Father are one."***

We talk more about the nature of Yeshua in the study, *'Manifestation of Elohim'* available on the Free Studies page at www.nazareneisrael.org. The question we need to be asking here, however, is that if Yeshua and His Father are one, and if YHWH the *Father* will not share His glory with any other, then why would Yeshua share His glory? Does it make any sense that the Lion of the Tribe of Judah would share His glory with a mortal human being? And if not, then what should we do with the prophecy at Genesis 49:24?

If Yeshua hypothetically returns at the start of the Millennium, to rule and reign supreme over the earth with a rod of iron, would He not have to share at least *some* of His power and glory with a man who earns the moniker, 'The Shepherd, the Stone of Israel?'

If a man from the Tribe of Joseph earns the name, 'The Shepherd, the Stone of Israel,' then surely he will have *some* kind of power and glory. However, if Yeshua returns at the start of the Millennium, to rule and reign supreme (and if He will not share His power or glory with another), then how can this man called 'The Shepherd, the Stone of Israel' ever earn his name? How can he earn this glory, if Yeshua has it all?

Further, what need would there be for a great national leader to arise from the Tribe of Joseph if Yeshua is already ruling and reigning supreme, sharing His power and glory with no man? Would it not be an insult to the Son of Elohim, to have to share his power and glory with a mortal human being?

What should we do in cases where we find a passage in prophecy that does not fit with Pre-Millennial Return Theory? Should we ignore that passage because it does not fit with our theory? Or should we abandon the theory instead?

What should we do with passages such as Hosea 2:2 (1:11 in English versions), which speaks of a national leader for combined twelve-tribe Israel, which cannot logically be Yeshua? Do we ignore that passage also?

The Book of Hosea was written primarily for the House of Israel (or Ephraim). It speaks of how Ephraim was scattered, how Ephraim would be regathered, and then re-united with his brothers in Judah.

Remembering that Kepha tells us that one prophetic day can represent a thousand earth years (2nd Peter 3:8), Hosea 6:2 tells us that the Ingathering of the Lost Ten Tribes of Israel (Ephraim) will take place some two thousand years after some special event.

> **Hoshea (Hosea) 6:2**
> **2 After two days He will revive us;**
> **On the third day He will raise us up,**
> **That we may live in His sight.**

As we explain in the *Nazarene Israel* book, that 'special event' was the advent of the Messiah, who was born on-or-about 4 BCE, and whose ministry lasted from approximately 26 to 29 CE. Two thousand years after His birth (i.e., 1996), the House of Ephraim began to re-assemble; and it seems likely that there will also be special events approximately two thousand years after His ministry and His resurrection (circa 2026-2029 CE). This is perfectly in keeping with the Hebraic conception of a Messiah: one who vanquishes Israel's enemies, and then brings the lost and scattered of Israel back to the eternal Covenant (the Torah). Yeshua is doing all of these things for His people (His Body), leading them by His Spirit.

Hosea 2:2 (1:11 in most English versions) speaks to the time when Yeshua's Spirit has brought the House of Israel (Ephraim) back together, and has even re-united them with their brothers in Judah (at the start of the Sabbath Millennium, Hosea 6:2). When we read this prophecy carefully, we see that it implies that combined Israel will *elect* a leader for themselves (which cannot logically be Yeshua). What it says, specifically, is that Judah and Israel (Ephraim) shall 'put' (i.e., appoint, or elect) one head for themselves.

Hosea 2:2	
2 Then the children of Judah and the children of Israel shall be gathered together, and appoint for themselves one head; and they shall come up out of the land, for great will be the day of Jezre'el!	(2) וְנִקְבְּצוּ בְּנֵי יְהוּדָה וּבְנֵי יִשְׂרָאֵל יַחְדָּו וְשָׂמוּ לָהֶם רֹאשׁ אֶחָד וְעָלוּ מִן הָאָרֶץ ׀ כִּי גָדוֹל יוֹם יִזְרְעֶאל׃

Proponents of a pre-millennial return insist that this passage refers to Yeshua. They say that when Yeshua returns to earth as the Conquering King (and the people are caught up to be with Him in the clouds), that all Israel will quite naturally want to follow Him. They will 'elect' Him, in that sense.

Once again, the pre-millennialist argument makes no sense. Zechariah 14 tells us that when Yeshua returns to earth, His feet will touch down on the Mount of Olives, splitting it in two.

Zechariah 14:3-4
3 Then YHWH will go forth and fight against those nations, as He fights in the day of battle.
4 And in that day His feet will stand on the Mount of Olives, which faces Jerusalem on the east; and the Mount of Olives shall be split in two, from east to west, making a very large valley. Half of the mountain shall move toward the north, and half of it toward the south.

This passage speaks of a very-much-larger-than-life-sized Yeshua. It speaks of a Yeshua so large that His feet will smash a small mountain (that is basically solid rock) in half. So when this very-much-larger-than-life-sized Yeshua returns to earth and His feet smash a solid rock mountain in half, are we going to stop and take an electoral vote, to see if we should appoint Him as our Head? And since Yeshua is not a respecter of persons in any way, why would He even care?

Picture it: the Conquering King stops, and allows His people to take a vote, to see whether they want to follow Him or not. Does it even make sense?

Consider the absurdity: In the day of His wrath, a man whose feet have just smashed a solid rock mountain in two will stop to recognize a popular vote? Just the thought of it would seem to make a mockery of His absolute power as a monarch.

So, since this elected (or 'appointed') head of Hosea 2:2 cannot logically be Yeshua, it must be a human; and now the same problem arises as before. If Yeshua comes at the start of the Millennium, to rule and reign supreme for a thousand years, then why would He share His power and glory with the man in Hosea 1:11?

This same problem crops up again in Jeremiah 30:6-9. Like most of the other passages we will mention, Jeremiah 30:6-9 speaks of the time of the Ingathering, and the re-establishment of a theological (religious) state in Israel.

In Jeremiah 30:6-9, there is to be a 'king' in Israel who is 'raised up' from among the people. Since this king is 'raised up' (rather than coming down from the clouds), this cannot be Yeshua.

> *Yirmeyahu (Jeremiah) 30:6-9*
> *6 Ask now, and see, whether a man is ever in labor with child? So why do I see every man with his hands on his loins like a woman in labor, and all faces turned pale?*
> *7 Alas! For that day is great, so that none is like it; and it is the time of Ya'akov's (Jacob's) trouble, but he shall be saved out of it.*
> *8 'For it shall come to pass in that day,' Says YHWH of hosts, 'That I will break his yoke from your neck, and will burst your bonds. Foreigners shall no more enslave them,*
> *9 But they shall serve YHWH their Elohim, and David their king, whom I will raise up for them.*

Who is David their king that is 'raised up' in this passage? We will talk more about spiritual resurrection later on in this book, but it cannot be Yeshua, for two reasons.

First, while Jeremiah was used to give this prophecy before the time of Yeshua's ministry, it speaks of a time that is still in the future. The king being mentioned here *will* be 'raised up' (future tense) whereas Yeshua has *already* been raised up (past tense).

Second, while "David their king" will be *raised up*, the Book of Acts tells us that when Yeshua returns, He will *come down* from the heavens (in a cloud).

Being 'raised up' is not the same thing as being brought back down, so let us take a look at Acts One.

> *Ma'asim (Acts) 1:9-11*
> *9 Now when He had spoken these things, while they watched, He was taken up, and a cloud received Him out of their sight.*
> *10 And while they looked steadfastly toward heaven as He went up, behold, two men stood by them in white apparel,*
> *11 who also said, "Men of Galilee, why do you stand gazing up into heaven? This same Yeshua, who was taken up from you into heaven, will so come in like manner as you saw Him go into heaven."*

So now we have the same question as before: If Yeshua returns in the clouds, but 'David their king' will be 'raised up,' then who is 'David their king'? And, if Yeshua will not share His power and glory with any man, is it possible that these men could co-exist?

Now, drop down a few verses to Jeremiah 30:18 (which still speaks about the time of the Ingathering, and the subsequent religious unification), and we will see yet another leader of the Nation of Israel, who also cannot logically be Yeshua.

> *Yirmeyahu (Jeremiah) 30:18-21*
> *18 "Thus says YHWH:*
> *'Behold, I will bring back the captivity of Ya'akov's tents, and have mercy on his dwelling places. The city shall be built upon its own mound, and the palace shall remain according to its own plan.*

19 Then out of them shall proceed thanksgiving and the voice of those who make merry; I will multiply them, and they shall not diminish; I will also glorify them, and they shall not be small.
20 Their children also shall be as before, and their congregation shall be established before Me; and I will punish all who oppress them.
21 Their leader shall come from among them, and their governor shall come from their midst. Then I will cause him to draw near, and he shall approach Me; for who is this who pledged his heart to approach Me?' says YHWH.

Verse twenty-one is mistranslated in many English versions, so let us look at it in the Hebrew. Here we find one man who is called to draw near to YHWH, who is referred to both as Israel's *leader*, and as Israel's *governor*. Since this man will come from the midst (rather than from the clouds) he cannot be Yeshua.

21 Their leader shall come from among them, and their governor shall come from their midst. Then I will cause him to draw near, and he shall approach Me; for who is this who pledged his heart to approach Me?' says YHWH.	(21) וְהָיָה אַדִּירוֹ מִמֶּנּוּ וּמֹשְׁלוֹ מִקִּרְבּוֹ יֵצֵא וְהִקְרַבְתִּיו וְנִגַּשׁ אֵלָי ׀ כִּי מִי הוּא זֶה עָרַב אֶת לִבּוֹ לָגֶשֶׁת אֵלַי נְאֻם יְהוָה

Next let us consider Zechariah 3:8.

The Orthodox Jews also agree that Zechariah 3:8 was fulfilled in Second Temple times (reference Ezra 3). However, since some verses seem to speak of future events, many Protestant and Messianic scholars believe that Zechariah 3:8 is still a future fulfillment.

Because so many Protestants and Messianics believe Zechariah 3:8 has not yet been fulfilled, let us assume (for the purposes of discussion) that Zechariah 3:8 is still to be fulfilled. It would nonetheless speak of persons who cannot be Yeshua, because as we shall soon see, more than one person wears a crown.

Zechariah 3:8	
8 'Hear, O Yehoshua, the high priest, you and your companions who sit before you, for they are a wondrous sign; for behold, I am bringing forth My servant the Branch.	(8) שְׁמַע נָא יְהוֹשֻׁעַ הַכֹּהֵן הַגָּדוֹל אַתָּה וְרֵעֶיךָ הַיֹּשְׁבִים לְפָנֶיךָ כִּי אַנְשֵׁי מוֹפֵת הֵמָּה ׀ כִּי הִנְנִי מֵבִיא אֶת עַבְדִּי צֶמַח

Many believers think that Yeshua is this 'Branch,' because Isaiah 11:1 tells us that a 'Branch' would come forth from the root of Jesse (King David's father).

1 There shall come forth a Rod from the stem of Jesse, and a Branch shall grow out of his roots.	(1) וְיָצָא חֹטֶר מִגֵּזַע יִשָׁי ׀ וְנֵצֶר מִשָּׁרָשָׁיו יִפְרֶה

45

The problem with this interpretation is that the reasoning is based on the English translations of the Hebrew, rather than on the Hebrew itself.

The word 'Branch' in Zechariah 3:8 is Tzemach (צֶמַח), whereas the word 'Branch' in Isaiah is Netzer (נֵצֶר). צֶמַח and נֵצֶר are completely different words; and yet because both of them translate to 'Branch' in English, Pre-Millennial Return Theory assumes that both of them refer to Yeshua. However, as we shall soon see, while Isaiah 11:1 does refer to Yeshua, Zechariah 3:8 does not.

Protestants and Messianics also tend to assume that Zechariah 3:8's reference to Yehoshua the High Priest is a reference to Yeshua, simply because we are told that Yeshua is our High Priest in the heavenly realms.

> *Ivrim (Hebrews) 8:1*
> *1 Now this is the main point of the things we are saying: We have such a High Priest, who is seated at the right hand of the throne of the Majesty in the heavens….*

Even assuming a future fulfillment, Yehoshua ben Yehotzedek is a different name than Yeshua ben Yosef (the Messiah). Further, just because Yeshua is our High Priest in the heavenly Tabernacle does not mean that Israel will never have another earthly (human) High Priest. In fact, if we read this passage closely, we should be able to see that Yehoshua the High Priest is not even one-in-the-same person as the 'Branch' (who will allegedly build Ezekiel's Temple). Zechariah 3:8 shows us that these are (or actually, were) two separate people.

> *Zechariah 3:8*
> *8 'Hear, O Yehoshua, the high priest, you and your companions who sit before you, for they are a wondrous sign; for behold, I am bringing forth My (other) servant, the Branch.*

Zechariah 6:11-13 clearly shows us that Yehoshua and the Branch are (or were) two separate persons, in that there are (or were) two crowns (plural), and a covenant of peace between both Yehoshua, and the Branch.

> *Zechariah 6:11-13*
> *11 Take the silver and gold, make an elaborate crown, and set it on the head of Yehoshua the son of Yehotzedek, the High Priest.*
> *12 Then speak to him, saying, 'Thus says YHWH of hosts, saying:*
> *"Behold, the (different) man whose name is the Branch: And he shall branch out from his place, and he shall build the temple of YHWH;*
> *13 Yes, he shall build the temple of YHWH. He shall bear the glory, and shall sit and rule on his throne; so he shall be a priest on his throne, and the counsel of peace shall be between them both."'*

If Yehoshua the son of Yehotzedek and the Branch will be one in the same person, then how can there be a counsel of peace between them *both*? Are the Pre-Millennial Return Theorists suggesting that Yeshua will actually be *two* separate human beings?

Now, assuming a future fulfillment, if Yeshua the Messiah hypothetically returns at the start of the Millennium, and if one of these two persons will be Yeshua, then who will the other person be? And why would they both wear crowns, if Yeshua is YHWH, and YHWH will not share His glory with another?

Moreover, if Yeshua the Messiah will allegedly be our next earthly High Priest, then why does Ezekiel 44:1-3 show us that next the high priest (here called 'the prince') will not be Yeshua? If we read this passage carefully, we should be able to see that the 'prince' being described here must be a mortal human being.

> *Yehezqel (Ezekiel) 44:1-3*
> *1 Then He brought me back to the outer gate of the sanctuary which faces toward the east, but it was shut.*
> *2 And YHWH said to me, "This gate shall be shut; it shall not be opened, and no man shall enter by it, because YHWH Elohim of Israel has entered by it; therefore it shall be shut.*
> *3 As for the prince, because he is the prince, he may sit in it to eat bread before YHWH; he shall enter by way of the vestibule of the gateway, and go out the same way."*

The pre-millennialist reads the word 'prince' in English and he says, "This prince must be Yeshua, because Isaiah 9:6 tells us that Yeshua is the Prince of Peace!" The only problem is that the word 'Prince' in Isaiah is a different Hebrew word.

The word 'prince' in Ezekiel 44:3 is 'Nah-see' (נָשִׂיא).

3 As for the prince (נָשִׂיא), because he is the prince, he may sit in it to eat bread before YHWH. He shall enter by way of the vestibule of the gateway, and go out the same way."	(3) אֶת הַנָּשִׂיא נָשִׂיא הוּא יֵשֶׁב בּוֹ לֶאֱכוֹל לֶחֶם לִפְנֵי יְהוָה ׀ מִדֶּרֶךְ אֵלָם הַשַּׁעַר יָבוֹא וּמִדַּרְכּוֹ יֵצֵא

In contrast, the word 'Prince' in Isaiah 9:5 (9:6 in most English versions) is 'Sar' (שַׂר).

Isaiah 9:5 5 For unto us a Child is born, unto us a Son is given; and the government will be upon His shoulder. And His name will be called Wonderful, Counselor, Mighty El, Everlasting Father, Prince of Peace.	(5) כִּי יֶלֶד יֻלַּד לָנוּ בֵּן נִתַּן לָנוּ וַתְּהִי הַמִּשְׂרָה עַל שִׁכְמוֹ ׀ וַיִּקְרָא שְׁמוֹ פֶּלֶא יוֹעֵץ אֵל גִּבּוֹר אֲבִיעַד שַׂר שָׁלוֹם

The 'prince' in Ezekiel cannot be Yeshua because he will be restricted from using the same gate that Yeshua used in the first century, because Yeshua used it.

> *2 And YHWH said to me, "This gate shall be shut; it shall not be opened, and no man shall enter by it, because YHWH Elohim of Israel has entered by it; therefore it shall be shut.*

> *3 As for the prince, because he is the prince, he may sit in it to eat bread before YHWH; he shall enter by way of the vestibule of the gateway, and go out the same way."*

Does it make sense that Yeshua will not be able to use the same gate that He used in the first century? Does it make sense that the Conquering King will only get to eat bread in the vestibule of the same gateway that He freely went in-and-out of in the first century, precisely because He went freely in-and-out of it, in the first century?

Moreover, Ezekiel 46:16-18 tells us that this 'prince' will have sons. Does that sound like Yeshua?

> *Yehezqel (Ezekiel) 46:16-18*
> *16 'Thus says YHWH Elohim: "If the prince gives a gift of some of his inheritance to any of his sons, it shall belong to his sons; it is their possession by inheritance.*
> *17 But if he gives a gift of some of his inheritance to one of his servants, it shall be his until the year of liberty, after which it shall return to the prince. But his inheritance shall belong to his sons; it shall become theirs.*
> *18 Moreover the prince shall not take any of the people's inheritance by evicting them from their property; he shall provide an inheritance for his sons from his own property, so that none of My people may be scattered from his property."'*

Since this prince is going to have sons, how can he be Yeshua? Do the pre-millennialists mean to tell us that the eternally glorified Son of the Living Elohim is going to take a mortal wife, and have mortal sons here on earth?

We have already seen that the word 'prince' here is 'nah-see' (נָשִׂיא). We should note, then, that in Hebrew the word 'nah-see' (נָשִׂיא) actually means something more like a president, prime minister or a governor (and not a king's son). The reason the word 'nah-see' (נָשִׂיא) is mistranslated as 'prince' in most English versions is that back when the King James Version was originally translated (in 1611), there was no such concept as 'president.' That office only came about some hundred-and-fifty years later, with the American Revolution. However, does it make any sense that Yeshua would have limited powers, like a president, a governor, or a prime minister would?

Notice also that this prince will offer up sacrifices on the Sabbaths, and on the New Moons.

> *Yehezqel (Ezekiel) 46:4-8*
> **4 The burnt offering that the prince offers to YHWH on the Sabbath day shall be six lambs without blemish, and a ram without blemish;**
> **5 and the grain offering shall be one ephah for a ram, and the grain offering for the lambs, as much as he wants to give, as well as a hin of oil with every ephah.**
> **6 On the day of the New Moon it shall be a young bull without blemish, six lambs, and a ram; they shall be without blemish.**

Since this prince must offer up sacrifices in Ezekiel's Temple, this prince will obviously have some kind of power and glory. However, now we are back to the exact same logical dilemma as before: since this is not Yeshua, if Yeshua were to return to earth at the start of the Millennium, then Yeshua would have to share some of His power and glory with this earthly prince (which would be against Isaiah 42:8).

So here we have eleven more witnesses (for a total of twelve so far) that show us that Yeshua cannot return at the start of the Millennium. And, we should add, there are many, many more examples.

But if Pre-Millennial Return Theory is unworkable, then is there a theory that tells us when the Messiah really will return? And does this theory tell us how the House of Ephraim will return back home to the Land of Israel, if not by supernatural means?

All thanks and praise to YHWH our Elohim, there is.

The Post-Millennial Model

Since we have seen that there are numerous logical flaws with the pre-millennial model, now let us take a look at the post-millennial model.

Once we understand that Yeshua must return at the end of the Millennium, we can then understand that Prophecy speaks of numerous prophetic milestones which must occur in the next several decades.

We do not know the exact dates and times these things will take place: and we do not need to know. However, Prophecy shows us that these prophetic milestones will take place in (at least more-or-less) the following order:

- A *spiritual* resurrection of the House of Joseph (taking place now, Ezekiel 37, 1st Cor. 15).
- Islamic attacks against the United States and Israel start the *War(s) for Territorial Expansion*.
- The United States and Israel emerge victorious from these wars (Zech. 10:5-10, Isaiah 11:14).
- At the conclusion of the *Wars for Territorial Expansion*, the annexation of lands creates a greatly expanded Land of Israel (Gen. 15:18).
- The Ingathering of the Lost Tribes fills these newly-annexed territories with Ephraimite settlers (Zech 9:6-7, Isa. 11:14-20, Isa. 66:20).
- The House of Judah sees that Yeshua is the reason the Ephraimites are coming back together as a nation, and accepts Yeshua as their Messiah (Zechariah 12:10).
- The Two Houses of Israel are united.

- Nazarene Israel is established as the official religion of all-twelve-tribe Israel.
- A combined government is established for all-twelve-tribe Israel (Hosea 2:2; [1:11 in English versions]).
- Tribulation comes at the *end* of the Millennium.
- Yeshua comes at-or-near the very *end* of the Tribulation, at the *last* trump, breaking the Mount of Olives in two (Zechariah 14).
- The saints are caught up to be with Yeshua in the air (1st Thessalonians 4:17).
- Yeshua takes His bride to the wedding feast at His Father's House (Revelation 21:9, etcetera).
- Those who pass the Judgment go to the New Heavens and the New Earth (Revelation 21, 22)

What this list of prophetic milestones shows, really, is how the Ephraimite people are supposed to unite, and then be used to provoke the House of Judah to jealousy for their Messiah; and how this will lead to the Ingathering. However, before the Ingathering can take place, first the House of Ephraim must unite, and the Kingdom of Ephraim must be rebuilt.

One of the reasons people like Pre-Millennial Return Theory so much is that it does not ask the believers to do anything together as His Body, in order for the Messiah to return. One can see why this theory would be popular, in that it would mean less work: but is this really what Scripture really says?

Alternately, is it possible that Scripture actually requires the Ephraimite people to undergo a kind of a *spiritual* resurrection, and begin functioning together as His Body once again, before the Messiah can return?

And is it possible that this *spiritual* resurrection is taking place even now? And is it even possible that the reason you are reading this book is because this spiritual resurrection is taking place in you, right now?

Is it possible that He is enacting a spiritual resurrection of the Ephraimite people, through the workings of His Spirit?

About Spiritual Resurrections

Why do we talk about a *spiritual* resurrection? After all, Yeshua was resurrected *physically* before ascending to His Father.

> *Yochanan (John) 20:24-28*
> *24 Now Thomas, called the Twin, one of the twelve, was not with them when Yeshua came.*
> *25 The other disciples therefore said to him, "We have seen the Master."*
> *So he said to them, "Unless I see in His hands the print of the nails, and put my finger into the print of the nails, and put my hand into His side, I will not believe."*
> *26 And after eight days His disciples were again inside, and Thomas with them. Yeshua came, the doors being shut, and stood in the midst, and said, "Peace to you!"*
> *27 Then He said to Thomas, "Reach your finger here, and look at My hands; and reach your hand here, and put it into My side. Do not be unbelieving, but believing."*
> *28 And Thomas answered and said to Him, "My Master and My Elohim!"*

It is also clear that Yeshua physically resurrected Lazarus from the dead.

> *Yochanan (John) 11:43-44*
> *43 Now when He had said these things, He cried with a loud voice, "Lazarus, come forth!"*
> *44 And he who had died came out bound hand and foot with graveclothes, and his face was wrapped with a cloth.*

So when the Renewed Covenant talks about *physical* resurrections, why should we talk of a *spiritual* one? One of the reasons is that the Apostle Shaul (Paul) tells us that there will be a mass resurrection that is *spiritual* in nature.

> *Qorintim Aleph (1st Cor.) 15:42-44*
> *42 So also is the resurrection of the dead. The body is sown in corruption, it is raised in incorruption.*
> *43 It is sown in dishonor, it is raised in glory. It is sown in weakness, it is raised in power.*
> *44 It is sown a natural body, it is raised a spiritual body.*

We will talk later about why we know Shaul is referring to Ezekiel 37 here. However, because most people do not think in spiritual terms, the concept of a *spiritual* resurrection seems foreign to them.

Still you may wonder, "What do we mean by the term, '*spiritual*' resurrection?" Yeshua tells us that there was a *kind* of a spiritual resurrection that took place in Yochanan haMatbil (John the Baptist), if we have ears to hear what Yeshua is really saying.

> *Mattai (Matthew) 11:11-15*
> *11 "Assuredly, I say to you, among those born of women there has not risen one greater than Yochanan haMatbil (John the Baptist); but he who is least in the kingdom of heaven is greater than he.*
> *12 And from the days of Yochanan haMatbil until now, the kingdom of heaven suffers violence, and the violent take it by force (i.e., the violent have overpowered Israel).*
> *13 For all the prophets and the Torah prophesied about Yochanan.*
> *14 And if you are willing to receive it, he is Eliyahu (Elijah) who is to come.*
> *15 He who has ears to hear, let him hear!"*

This can be a difficult question to understand, but was Yochanan haMatbil (John the Baptist) *literally* Eliyahu HaNavi? No, of course he was not. Yochanan was Yochanan (not some 'reincarnation' of Eliyahu).

However, did Yochanan haMatbil come *in the spirit of* Eliyahu? Yes, the Scripture plainly says that he would, and this is precisely what happened.

> *Luqa (Luke) 1:13-17*
> *13 But the messenger (angel) said to him, "Do not be afraid, Zachariah, for your prayer is heard; and your wife Elisheva will bear you a son, and you shall call his name Yochanan (John).*
> *14 And you will have joy and gladness, and many will rejoice at his birth.*

> *15 For he will be great in the sight of YHWH, and shall drink neither wine nor strong drink. He will also be filled with the Set-apart Spirit, even from his mother's womb. 16 And he will turn many of the children of Israel to YHWH their Elohim.*
>
> *17 He will also go before Him in the spirit and power of Elijah, 'to turn the hearts of the fathers to the children,' and the disobedient to the wisdom of the just, to make ready a people prepared for YHWH."*

So if Yochanan haMatbil came in the spirit and power of Eliyahu, then is there anyone else who ever came in the spirit and power of Eliyahu? Yes: Scripture tells us that the prophet Elisha did also.

> *Melachim Bet (2nd Kings) 2:9-15*
> *9 And so it was, when they had crossed over, that Elijah said to Elisha, "Ask! What may I do for you, before I am taken away from you?"*
> *Elisha said, "Please let a double portion of your spirit be upon me."*
> *10 So he said, "You have asked a hard thing. Nevertheless, if you see me when I am taken from you, it shall be so for you; but if not, it shall not be so." 11 Then it happened, as they continued on and talked, that suddenly a chariot of fire appeared with horses of fire, and separated the two of them; and Elijah went up by a whirlwind into heaven.*

12 And Elisha saw it, and he cried out, "My father, my father, the chariot of Israel and its horsemen!" So he saw him no more. And he took hold of his own clothes and tore them into two pieces.
13 He also took up the mantle of Elijah that had fallen from him, and went back and stood by the bank of the Jordan.
14 Then he took the mantle of Elijah that had fallen from him, and struck the water, and said, "Where is YHWH Elohim of Elijah?"
And when he also had struck the water, it was divided this way and that; and Elisha crossed over.
15 Now when the sons of the prophets who were from Jericho saw him, they said, "The spirit of Elijah rests on Elisha." And they came to meet him, and bowed to the ground before him.

First Eliyahu had his own spirit, and then Elisha had it, and then finally, Yochanan haMatbil had Eliyahu's spirit. Does this mean that Eliyahu was 'reincarnated'? No, not at all! What happened was that both Elisha and Yochanan haMatbil were given the spirit of Eliyahu. That is to say that YHWH caused the spirit of Eliyahu to *rest upon* them (or *in* them, as the case may be). They were given Eliyahu's spirit.

If this concept seems foreign, just sit with it for a while. However, for people to be 'given' other spirits is by no means a new concept in Scripture. The Tanach (the 'Old' Covenant) gives us many other examples of this.

For example, the Spirit of Elohim dwelt in Joseph.

> ***B'reisheet (Genesis) 41:38***
> **38 And Pharaoh said to his servants, "Can we find such a one as this, a man in whom is the Spirit of Elohim?"**

That the Spirit of Elohim dwelt *in* Joseph did **not** mean that Joseph *was* YHWH any more than Elisha *was* Eliyahu: rather, what happened was that Joseph died to his own fleshly will (and his thoughts), so that he could hear, speak and act according to the Still Small Voice (which is what prophesying is).

Even Bala'am, the son of Be'or was given His Spirit!

> ***Bemidbar (Numbers) 24:2***
> **2 And Balaam raised his eyes, and saw Israel encamped according to their tribes; and the Spirit of Elohim came upon him.**

We could also note that Yehoshua (Joshua) the son of Nun was filled with a 'Spirit of Wisdom.'

> ***Devarim (Deuteronomy) 34:9***
> **9 Now Yehoshua (Joshua) the son of Nun was full of the spirit of wisdom, for Moshe had laid his hands on him; so the children of Israel heeded him, and did as YHWH had commanded Moshe.**

The Spirit of YHWH came upon King Shaul.

> *Shemu'El Aleph (1st Samuel) 10:6*
> *6 Then the Spirit of YHWH will come upon you, and you will prophesy with them, and be turned into another man.*

However, the Spirit of YHWH was also *taken* from King Shaul, and YHWH sent a distressing spirit to replace it.

> *Shemu'El Aleph (1st Samuel) 16:14-15*
> *14 But the Spirit of YHWH departed from Shaul, and a distressing spirit from YHWH troubled him.*
> *15 And Shaul's servants said to him, "Surely, a distressing spirit from Elohim is troubling you!"*

We can also see that spirits are not limited to being placed on (or in) certain individuals; but even groups of people can have certain 'spirits.' For example, Hosea 4:12 tells us that the House of Israel (Ephraim) has a *Spirit of Harlotry*. This is because idolatry is spiritual adultery, and the Ephraimites are idolaters in that they worship on wrong days (e.g., Sunday, Christmas).

> *Hosea 4:12*
> *12 My people ask counsel from their wooden idols, and their staff informs them; for the spirit of harlotry has caused them to stray, and they have played the harlot against their Elohim.*

It could also be said that the House of Judah has a 'spirit of anti-Messiah,' while the House of Ephraim has had a 'spirit of rebellion' and/or a 'spirit of anti-Torah.'

As we will see, YHWH promises to cleanse Ephraim of her idolatry, and to punish her severely for not keeping *all* of His Torah. Similarly, Isaiah tells us that YHWH will wash away the filth of the daughters of Zion, and purge the blood of Jerusalem from her midst, by a *Spirit of Judgment,* and a *Spirit of Burning.*

> **Yeshayahu (Isaiah) 4:4-5**
> **4 When YHWH has washed away the filth of the daughters of Zion, and purged the blood of Jerusalem from her midst, by the Spirit of Judgment and by the Spirit of Burning,**
> **5 then YHWH will create above every dwelling place of Mount Zion, and above her assemblies, a cloud and smoke by day and the shining of a flaming fire by night; for over all the glory there will be a covering.**

Judah will also be cleansed by YHWH's '*Spirit of Favor* ("grace") *and Supplication.*'

> **Zechariah 12:10**
> **10 "And I will pour on the House of David and on the inhabitants of Jerusalem the Spirit of grace and supplication; then they will look on Me whom they pierced. Yes, they will mourn for Him as one mourns for his only son, and grieve for Him as one grieves for a firstborn.**

In a certain sense, these 'spirits' refer to our attitudes, our mindsets, our predispositions, and our inclinations.

In the spiritual realm, these spirits are real beings, and the more advanced practitioners among us can not only spot them, but can also name them (as well as cast them out). For example, the apostles were able to name the evil spirits that Yeshua cast out.

> *Luqa (Luke) 4:32-36*
> *32 And they were astonished at His teaching, for His word was with authority.*
> *33 Now in the synagogue there was a man who had a spirit of an unclean demon. And he cried out with a loud voice, 34 saying, "Let us alone! What have we to do with You, Yeshua of Nazareth? Did You come to destroy us? I know who You are — the Set-apart One of Elohim!"*
> *35 But Yeshua rebuked him, saying, "Be quiet, and come out of him!" And when the demon had thrown him in their midst, it came out of him and did not hurt him.*
> *36 Then they were all amazed and spoke among themselves, saying, "What a word this is! For with authority and power He commands the unclean spirits, and they come out!"*

If someone without eyes to see were to encounter a man like this in a synagogue today, he might say, "That man has a really bad attitude!" That is because, to eyes that are not trained to see, evil spirits can *look* like a bad attitude (because they give one a bad attitude). However, Yeshua understood that the root problem was not just a bad attitude, but an evil *spirit*.

It can be a challenge for Westerners to realize that the material world is not the primary reality; but that the spiritual world is actually the more fundamental reality. This shift is challenging, but important to make.

Do we honestly believe that evil spirits are only a thing of the past; and that they ceased to exist after the first century? Do we honestly believe that we do not have to deal with evil spirits in today's times? Or are we willing to re-assess the spiritual landscape in front of us with eyes that can see (and discern) evil spirits?

The Apostle Shaul also discerned evil spirits when he encountered them, and he treated them as such.

> *Ma'asim (Acts) 16:16-18*
> *16 Now it happened, as we went to prayer, that a certain slave girl possessed with a spirit of divination met us, who brought her masters much profit by fortune-telling.*
> *17 This girl followed Shaul and us, and cried out, saying, "These men are the servants of the Most High Elohim, who proclaim to us the way of salvation."*
> *18 And this she did for many days. But Shaul, greatly annoyed, turned and said to the spirit, "I command you in the Name of Yeshua HaMashiach to come out of her." And he came out that very hour.*

If this were to happen in modern times, someone might refer the girl to a psychologist, or to a psychiatrist (for medications). However, when Shaul recognized he was dealing with an unclean spirit, he simply cast it out.

We will talk elsewhere about how to cast demons out. However, the thing to notice here is that the *Hebrew* apostles understood that the way to deal with the material world was not superficially, but in the spirit. Since they were dealing with spiritual issues, they had to deal with things at the spiritual level.

> *Qorintim Aleph (1st Cor.) 2:14-15*
> **14 But the natural man does not receive the things of the Spirit of Elohim, for they are foolishness to him; nor can he know them, because they are spiritually discerned.**

If we have eyes to read, we should be able to see that the Renewed Covenant is full of spiritual things. Yochanan tells us that the apostles could even tell who was *really* of Elohim (and who was not) by whether or not they heard and understood their (real) message.

> *Yochanan Aleph (1st John) 4:5-6*
> **5 They are of the world. Therefore they speak as of the world, and the world hears them.**
> **6 We are of Elohim. He who knows Elohim hears us; he who is not of Elohim does not hear us. By this we know the Spirit of Truth and the Spirit of Error.**

Yochanan is telling us that the apostles knew who had a love for the truth, and who did not. Those who had been given the *Spirit of Truth* could understand the truths the apostles were saying; whereas those with the Spirit of Error could not.

Let's read this again.

> **Yochanan Aleph (1ˢᵗ John) 4:5-6**
> **5 They are of the world. Therefore they speak as of the world, and the world hears them.**
> **6 We are of Elohim. He who knows Elohim hears us; he who is not of Elohim does not hear us. By this we know the Spirit of Truth and the Spirit of Error.**

If you understand the truths we are speaking here, then at least to some degree, you have been given (and have received) the *Spirit of Truth*. You read the words we write, and you recognize the truth in them. Without having been given at least some measure of His *Spirit of Truth*, you could not do this.

Similarly, for those of us who are of the House of Joseph (Ephraim), unless YHWH had first restored our Ephraimite spirits to us, how could we have known that we are Ephraimites? The fact is that we can only know that we are Ephraimites because our Ephraimite spirits have been *spiritually* resurrected.

The reason we now have Ephraimite spirits is because Elohim has restored these Ephraimite spirits to us. He has renewed these spirits within us, in accordance with His promise to spiritually resurrect the House of Israel (which we will talk about in the next chapter).

In Ezekiel 36 (just prior to the promise of the spiritual resurrection), YHWH describes this exact same event in a different way. He promises to put a 'new spirit' within us; and *then* bring us back to His Land.

> *Yehezqel (Ezekiel) 36:24-28*
> *24 For I will take you from among the nations, gather you out of all countries, and bring you into your own land.*
> *25 <u>Then</u> I will sprinkle clean water on you, and you shall be clean; I will cleanse you from all your filthiness and from all your idols.*
> *26 I will give you a new heart and put a new spirit within you; I will take the heart of stone out of your flesh and give you a heart of flesh.*
> *27 I will put My Spirit within you and cause you to walk in My statutes, and you will keep My judgments and do them.*
> *28 <u>Then</u> you shall dwell in the land that I gave to your fathers; you shall be My people, and I will be your Elohim.*

The specific language of this passage is important. Remembering that sequence matters when interpreting prophecy, verses 24 and 25 tell us that *first* YHWH will bring us back to His Land, and *then* He will sprinkle clean water on us (and we shall be clean). However, verses 26 through 28 tell us just the opposite: that *first* YHWH will put a new spirit within us, and *then* He will bring us back to His Land.

So which is it? Is YHWH contradicting Himself? Do we receive a new spirit before we come back to His Land? Or do we receive a new spirit *after* we come back to His Land? Or are perhaps both true?

As we will see, both are true.

Elsewhere in prophecy, YHWH tells us that first He will give us a new spirit, and *then* He will bring us back to His Land (at the time of the Ingathering). Then, other passages tell us that *after* He brings us back to His Land, *then* He will give us even more of His Spirit.

Just a few verses later, Ezekiel 36:31-32 shows us that while some believers may receive the fullness of His Spirit prior to the Ingathering (in that they work hard for their Elohim, and submit themselves completely to His Voice), the majority of Ephraim will not receive the fullness of His Spirit until after the Ingathering is already over.

> *Yehezqel (Ezekiel) 36:31-32*
> *31 <u>Then</u> you will remember your evil ways and your deeds that were not good; and you will loathe yourselves in your own sight, for your iniquities and your abominations.*
> *32 Not for your sake do I do this," says YHWH Elohim, "let it be known to you. Be ashamed and confounded for your own ways, O House of Israel!"*

This passage tells us that Ephraim will come home in a less-than-pure state, not having fully repented.

If we reflect on this, we can see a mystery: YHWH says He will bring His people back to His Land, even *before* we have received the fullness of His Spirit.

But how is that possible? How can we return back to His Land if we do not have the fullness of His Spirit? Why would anyone even *want* to go back to the Land of Israel if he does not have the fullness of His Spirit?

We will explain why the Ephraimites will want to come back home (even in their impure state) in the chapter entitled, *"The Wars of Territorial Expansion."* However, before we can talk about the coming war with Islam, we need to discuss Ezekiel 37, because it will reveal much about the great mission that lies ahead of the Ephraimite people, if they are to be used to provoke Judah to jealousy (so that he accepts his Messiah).

However, before we can talk about Ezekiel 37, first we must explain the Post Millennial Rapture, also called the *'Great Catching Away.'*

That is, ironically, before we can talk about the First Resurrection, first we must talk about the second one. The reason for this is that most people only understand the Second Resurrection, and once we understand what the Second Resurrection really is, then they can understand what it really is not.

Once we understand what the Second Resurrection is not, then we can begin to understand what the First Resurrection really is, and why it is taking place even now, as you read this book.

The Second Resurrection

Even though Yeshua raised people physically from the dead, First Corinthians Fifteen speaks of a mass resurrection that is *spiritual* (not physical).

> *Qorintim Aleph (1st Cor.) 15:42-44*
> *42 So also is the resurrection of the dead. The body is sown in corruption, it is raised in incorruption.*
> *43 It is sown in dishonor, it is raised in glory. It is sown in weakness, it is raised in power.*
> *44 It is sown a natural body, it is raised a spiritual body.*

In fact, Scripture describes not just one mass spiritual resurrection, but two. Perhaps ironically, we need to discuss the Second Resurrection first (in this chapter), and then the first one (in the next chapter).

The second great mass spiritual resurrection is the '*Great Catching Away*' (also called the '*Post-Millennial Rapture*'). As we will see here, this event takes place at the end (not the beginning) of the Millennium. Shaul describes this event in First Thessalonians 4:13-18.

> *1st Thessalonians 4:13-17*
> *13 But I do not want you to be ignorant, brethren, concerning those who have fallen asleep, lest you sorrow as others who have no hope.*

> *14 For if we believe that Yeshua died and rose again, even so Elohim will bring with Him those who sleep in Yeshua.*
> *15 For this we say to you by the word of the Master, that we who are alive and remain until the coming of the Master will by no means precede those who are asleep.*
> *16 For the Master Himself will descend from heaven with a shout, with the voice of an archangel, and with the trumpet of Elohim. And the dead in Messiah will rise first.*
> *17 Then we who are alive and remain shall be caught up together with them in the clouds to meet Master in the air. And thus we shall always be with the Master.*

Verse 16 tells us that when Yeshua descends from heaven "with the trumpet of Elohim," we who are left alive will be caught up to meet Him in the air.

This same event is also described in 1st Corinthians 15:52 (below). Here Shaul tells us that Yeshua will return at the *Last* Trumpet (i.e., at the end of earth's history). Please note that Shaul does not say Yeshua returns a thousand years *before* the Last Trumpet: rather, He returns *at* the Last Trumpet.

> *Qorintim Aleph (1st Cor) 15:50-54*
> *50 Now this I say, brethren, that flesh and blood cannot inherit the kingdom of Elohim; nor does corruption inherit incorruption.*

> *51 Behold, I tell you a mystery: We shall not all sleep, but we shall all be changed —*
> *52 in a moment, in the twinkling of an eye, at the last trumpet. For the (last) trumpet will sound, and the dead will be raised incorruptible, and we shall be changed.*
> *53 For this corruptible must put on incorruption, and this mortal must put on immortality.*
> *54 So when this corruptible has put on incorruption, and this mortal has put on immortality, then shall be brought to pass the saying that is written: "Death is swallowed up in victory."*

The reason our bodies will be changed is that this is the time of the earth's destruction; and then we all go to the Day of Judgment. This is also the same time frame spoken of in Revelation 20:7-11.

> *Gilyana (Revelation) 20:7-11*
> *7 Now when the thousand years have expired, Satan will be released from his prison*
> *8 and will go out to deceive the nations which are in the four corners of the earth, Gog and Magog, to gather them together to battle, whose number is as the sand of the sea.*
> *9 They went up on the breadth of the earth and surrounded the camp of the saints and the beloved city. And fire came down from Elohim out of heaven and devoured them.*

> **10 The devil, who deceived them, was cast into the lake of fire and brimstone where the beast and the false prophet are. And they will be tormented day and night forever and ever.**
> **11 Then I saw a great white throne and Him who sat on it, from whose face the earth and the heaven fled away. And there was found no place for them.**

Notice this passage gives us the following sequence:

1. *First* comes the thousand years;
2. *Then* comes the War of Gog and Magog (at the end of the thousand years, verse 7);
3. Then the War of Gog and Magog ends when Yeshua calls fire down out of heaven upon the armies of Satan (verse 9, explained below).
4. The heavens and earth flee away from the One who sits on the great white throne (in the Day of Wrath/Day of Judgment, verse 11).

We know it will be Yeshua who will call down fire out of the heavens to destroy the armies of Satan, because it sounds exactly like what happened in the days of Sodom and Gomorrah.

> **B'reisheet (Genesis) 19:24**
> **24 Then YHWH rained brimstone and fire on Sodom and Gomorrah, from YHWH out of the heavens.**

[For more details as to why this is Yeshua, please see the study, 'Manifestation of Elohim.']

Notice that Scripture does not speak of a thousand-year period of time in between the destruction of Satan's armies at the War of Gog and Magog, and the Day of Judgment. Rather, it seems to indicate that there is only a relatively short period of years.

> *Gilyana (Revelation) 20:9-11*
> *9 They went up on the breadth of the earth and surrounded the camp of the saints and the beloved city. And fire came down from Elohim out of heaven and devoured them.*
> *10 The devil, who deceived them, was cast into the lake of fire and brimstone where the beast and the false prophet are. And they will be tormented day and night forever and ever.*
> *11 Then I saw a great white throne and Him who sat on it, from whose face the earth and the heaven fled away. And there was found no place for them.*

While the exact sequence of events is not known at this time, earth and heaven flee away from the great white throne at the Day of Judgment, because this is when a much larger-than-life-sized Yeshua has come to destroy the earth in the Day of Vengeance. Thankfully, a loving and merciful Yeshua catches His bride up to be with Him in this Day of Vengeance, even as he lands His feet down on the Mount of Olives, smashing this mountain of solid rock in half.

> *Zechariah 14:3-4*
> *3 Then YHWH will go forth and fight against those nations, as He fights in the day of battle.*

> *4 And in that day His feet will stand on the Mount of Olives, which faces Jerusalem on the east; and the Mount of Olives shall be split in two, from east to west, making a very large valley. Half of the mountain shall move toward the north, and half of it toward the south.*

The time that the earth is destroyed is called by many names. It is called the Day of YHWH, the Day of His Wrath, the Day of Vengeance, the Second Coming, and so forth. In order to know what will happen in that day, we should also consider Kepha's (Peter's) prophecy in 2nd Peter 3:10-13 once again.

> *Kepha Bet (2nd Peter) 3:10-13*
> *10 But the Day of YHWH will come as a thief in the night, in which the heavens will pass away with a great noise, and the elements will melt with fervent heat; both the earth and the works that are in it will be burned up.*
> *11 Therefore, since all these things will be dissolved, what manner of persons ought you to be in set-apart conduct and set-apartness,*
> *12 looking for and hastening the coming of the day of Elohim, because of which the heavens will be dissolved, being on fire, and the elements will melt with fervent heat?*
> *13 Nevertheless we, according to His promise, look for new heavens and a new earth in which righteousness dwells.*

In Verse 10, Kepha tells us that when Yeshua returns, the heavens will pass away with a great noise, the elements will melt with a fervent heat, and both the earth and the works that are in it will be burned up. So the question we ought to ask ourselves is this: If the heavens will be dissolved in the Day of Yeshua's return (being on fire, verse 12), then how can Yeshua return at the start of the Millennium? What would be left for Him to rule and reign over?

We also know that the Apostles equated Yeshua's return with the time of the end of the world.

> *Mattai (Matthew) 24:3*
> *3 And as He sat upon the Mount of Olives, the disciples came unto him privately, saying, "Tell us, when shall these things be?" and, "what shall be the sign of thy coming, and of the end of the world (end of everything)?"*

The word 'world' here is often mistranslated as 'age.' However, the word in Hebrew would have been 'olam' (עוֹלָם), which in this context would mean 'everything.' Therefore, the Apostles understood that Yeshua's return would be at the end of the world as we know it.

Further, if we understand the Hebrew mindset, we can even see evidence for the *Post-Millennial Rapture* (or the post-millennial *Great Catching Away*) in the picture of the ancient Jewish wedding ceremony.

In the ancient Jewish wedding ceremony, a bridegroom 'takes' (or 'engages') his bride, and then he goes off to his father's house, to prepare a place for them both to live. Notice that Yeshua also said He would do this.

> *Yochanan (John) 14:2-3*
> *2 In My Father's house are many mansions. If it were not so, I would have told you. I go to prepare a place for you.*
> *3 And if I go and prepare a place for you, I will come again and receive you to Myself; that where I am, there you may be also.*

When the groom has prepared a house for his bride and the wedding supper is all perfectly prepared, the father then sends his son to bring his new bride home. Out of courtesy, the bridegroom usually sends his friend ahead of him, to alert the bride's father that he will come and take his new bride about midnight.

The bridegroom then comes 'as a thief in the night,' but he blows the shofar to initiate a mock battle between himself and the bride's father and brothers, who (of course) lose this mock battle to the groom. And so it is that after 'vanquishing' the bride's family, the groom then spirits his bride back to his father's house, where the wedding supper will be held the following evening.

Notice how beautifully all of this fits with the idea of a Post-Millennial Return: Yeshua returns as a thief in the night, with the sound of a great shofar. Then there is a (basically) staged battle between Yeshua and the bride's father (i.e., Satan) and the bride's father's sons (i.e., the armies of Gog and Magog). Yeshua wins this mock battle, and takes His bride back home.

This also fits with the parable of the Ten Virgins, in which Yeshua takes all the virgins who have prepared themselves for His arrival, to go and be with Him.

> *Mattai (Matthew) 25:6-10*
> *6 "And at midnight a cry was heard: 'Behold, the bridegroom is coming; go out to meet him!'*
> *7 Then all those virgins arose and trimmed their lamps.*
> *8 And the foolish said to the wise, 'Give us some of your oil, for our lamps are going out.'*
> *9 But the wise answered, saying, 'No, lest there should not be enough for us and you; but go rather to those who sell, and buy for yourselves.'*
> *10 And while they went to buy, the bridegroom came, and those who were ready went in with him to the wedding; and the door was shut."*

Notice that in this parable, there is no thousand-year wait in between the coming of the bridegroom, and the wedding feast. Rather, the groom takes all those who are ready (while everyone else gets left behind).

Notice, then, that at least according to Pre-Millennial Return Theory, Yeshua comes back to earth at the start of the Millennium, and then hangs around the bride's house (i.e., the earth) for a thousand years before taking her (Israel) back to His Father's House. The wedding supper goes stale, and the Father starts to wonder what has happened to His Son.

Think about it: If you were Yeshua, would *you* want to hang around the bride's father's house for a thousand years? Or would you rather take your bride (Israel) straight back to your Father's House, so you could begin enjoying your new life together right away?

Pre-Millennial Return Theory is a beautiful theory that just does not work. The reason it survives is because so many people desperately *want* it to be true; and because so many people have not eyes to see that it asks us to believe things that just can never be.

Isn't it time people stopped trying to make Scripture say what *they* want it to say? Isn't it time just to step back, and take a really good look at what Scripture actually *does* say (and then believe that, instead)?

The First Resurrection

The Book of Genesis is generally considered prophetic, in that the events which are recorded in Genesis foreshadow events that later recur in Scripture (as well as in history). Notice, then, that Genesis Fifty records how the patriarch Yosef (Joseph) made the children of Israel promise to bring his bones with them, when they came to the Promised Land.

> **B'reisheet (Genesis) 50:25**
> **25 Then Yosef took an oath from the children of Israel, saying, "Elohim will surely visit you, and you shall carry up my bones (עַצְמֹתַי) from here."**

Then, when Moshe (Moses) led the first exodus, he did bring Yosef's bones (עַצְמֹתַי) with him.

> **Shemote (Exodus) 13:19**
> **19 And Moshe took the bones (עַצְמֹתַי) of Yosef with him, for he had placed the children of Israel under solemn oath, saying, "Elohim will surely visit you, and you shall carry up my bones from here with you."**

But why does Scripture tell us that Yosef made the children of Israel swear to bring his bones up out of Egypt? Was it just that he wanted to be buried in the Promised Land? Or was there something more?

In the *Nazarene Israel* study, we show how the House of Israel (Ephraim) is represented by the patriarch Yosef. Accordingly, that a Melchizedekian priest such as Moshe HaNavi would bring Yosef's bones out of Egypt perfectly symbolizes what is beginning to take place in the present day, with the first resurrection.

Scripture tells us that the life is in the blood.

> ***Vayiqra (Leviticus) 17:11***
> ***11 For the life of the flesh is in the blood, and I have given it to you upon the altar to make atonement for your souls; for it is the blood that makes atonement for the soul.'***

While the life is in the blood, blood is created in the bone marrow. By extension, then, we ought to be able to see that life is 'regenerated' in the bone marrow. What is so interesting, then, is that the eastern medical arts (such as Chinese Medicine) tell us that a person's bones are a kind of a repository for their spirit.

Westerners often have difficulty accepting the fact that the Israelite faith is an eastern (and not a Western) faith, just as the Land of Israel lies in the Middle East (and not in the Mid-West). Eastern symbolism is used all throughout Scripture, from Genesis to Revelation, and also here in Ecclesiastes.

> ***Qohelet (Ecclesiastes) 12:6-7***
> ***6 Remember your Creator before the silver cord is loosed, or the golden bowl is broken, or the pitcher shattered at the fountain, or the wheel broken at the well.***

> **7 Then the dust will return to the earth as it was, and the spirit will return to Elohim who gave it.**

In Hebraic thought, the spinal cord is sometimes called the 'silver' cord, while the skull is called the 'golden bowl,' and etceteras. The meanings of these Hebraic symbols are lost on most readers, however, because most readers read with Western eyes. The average Western reader is therefore confused about the meaning and symbolism of bones in Hebraic thought.

Notice that the righteous King Josiah exhumed and burned the bones of false priests, as a punishment for their having sinned against YHWH. Why?

> **Divre HaYamim (2nd Chronicles) 34:5**
> **5 He (Josiah) also burned the bones of the priests on their altars, and (he) cleansed Judah and Jerusalem.**

In eastern thought, by burning their bones (עֲצָמוֹת), Josiah was effectively condemning these false priests forever. This is because to burn someone's bones is to destroy any opportunity that they may have for spiritual renewal or regeneration (i.e., spiritual resurrection).

Understand: Since YHWH is completely sovereign, He can assuredly resurrect anyone to spiritual life that He wants, whether their bones have been burned or not. For example, if a devout believer was cremated, this is not necessarily the end for them. However, we should consider this eastern concept of bones-as-repositories-for-the-personal-spirit when we read the so-called 'Dry Bones Resurrection' of Ezekiel 37.

In verse one of Ezekiel 37 we find that special phrase, "in the Spirit." This phrase alerts us to the fact that we must be careful to understand that what we are about to read is not to be taken literally. Rather, we are about to read a purely symbolic *vision*.

> **Yehezqel (Ezekiel) 37:1-14**
> **1 The hand of YHWH came upon me and brought me out in the Spirit of YHWH, and set me down in the midst of the valley; and it was full of bones.**
> **2 Then He caused me to pass by them all around, and behold, there were very many in the open valley; and indeed they were very dry.**

When we read "in the Spirit" about a valley whose face is covered with bones that are "very dry," we should understand that this passage is speaking in symbolism. It must be symbolism that is being spoken here, because there is no valley here on earth whose face is literally covered with "very dry" bones (עֲצָמוֹת).

As we will see below (in verse eleven), these bones are symbolic of the bones (the spiritual repositories) of the whole House of Israel (Ephraim). The reason these spiritual bones are so 'dry' is that the Ephraimite people have been spiritually dead for the past 2,730 years.

As we explain in *Nazarene Israel*, when the House of Ephraim was taken into the Dispersion, they did not die out physically. Rather, it was just that their children no longer thought of themselves as Ephraimites; and so their Ephraimite *spirits* died. Then, since they were no longer distinguishable from the rest of the gentiles, the Jews ruled that they should be called 'gentiles.'

However, it is not as if the Ephraimite people *physically* died out, and 'gentile Christians' have replaced them. Rather, the physical descendants of Ephraim live on, albeit with a tremendous amount of in-and-out-grafting. However, since we are still dealing with the physical (and prophetic) descendants of Ephraim, all that is really needed is a renewing (or a *resurrection*) of the House of Ephraim's *spirits*; and Ephraim will live again.

This, then, is precisely why Ezekiel 37 speaks of a *spiritual* resurrection (or 'renewal.')

> *3a And He said to me, "Son of man, can these bones (עֲצָמוֹת) live?"*
> *3b So I answered, "O YHWH Elohim, You know!"*

YHWH knows Ephraim's dry bones can live, because He plans to renew them (or *resurrect* them) spiritually. That is, YHWH says He will renew the spirits in the descendants of Ephraim all over the world (whether they are of literal or ingrafted descent): and if we take a good look around us at the world, we can see that this is (in fact) what is taking place even now.

> *4 Again He said to me, "Prophesy to these bones, and say to them, 'O dry bones, hear the word of YHWH!*
> *5 Thus says YHWH Elohim to these bones: Surely I will cause breath to enter into you, and you shall live.*
> *6 I will put sinews on you and bring flesh upon you, cover you with skin and put breath in you; and you shall live. Then you shall know that I am YHWH."'*

In Hebrew, the word for *breath* is the same as the word for *spirit*: "ruach" (רוח): there is no difference. So, when YHWH tells us that He will cause breath (רוח) to enter into the dry bones, He is also telling us (at the exact same time) that He will breathe a new spirit (רוח) into the House of Ephraim: it is the same event.

> **7 So I prophesied as He commanded me; and as I prophesied, there was a noise, and suddenly a rattling; and the bones came together, bone to bone.**
> **8 Indeed, as I looked, the sinews and the flesh came upon them, and the skin covered them over; but there was no breath in them.**

First there was a noise, as some people started talking about the Two Houses of Israel. Then there was a rattling, as people began talking about re-organizing, so we can go back home to the Land. Now the leaders are beginning to join together, bone to bone; and soon His Body will be covered with sinews and skin, as people begin to understand that we need to obey the whole Torah (and not just a part of it). As this process continues, His Body will slowly be reformed.

> **9 Also He said to me, "Prophesy to the breath, prophesy, son of man, and say to the breath, 'Thus says YHWH Elohim: "Come from the four winds, O breath, and breathe on these slain, that they may live."'"**
> **10 So I prophesied as He commanded me, and breath came into them, and they lived, and stood upon their feet, an exceedingly great army.**

Verse ten tells us that as our nation continues to be reformed, we will be turned into an exceedingly great army. Notice, however, that to be an army requires one to have structure, discipline, accountability, and a purpose.

In contrast, Pre-Millennial Return Theory informs us that it would be wrong of us to form ourselves into an army (even though Ezekiel 37 requires it). Rather, Pre-Millennial Return Theory tells us that we should just be patient, and keep on waiting for Yeshua to bring us back to the Land of Israel by supernatural means.

> *11 Then He said to me, "Son of man, these bones are the whole House of Israel. They indeed say, 'Our bones are dry, our hope is lost, and we ourselves are cut off!'*
> *12 Therefore prophesy and say to them, 'Thus says YHWH Elohim: "Behold, O My people, I will open your graves and cause you to come up from your graves, and bring you into the land of Israel.*
> *13 Then you shall know that I am YHWH, when I have opened your graves, O My people, and brought you up from your graves.*

YHWH tells us that it is *He* who will cause us to come up from our graves, and that it is *He* who will bring us back to the Land of Israel by the leading and guiding of His Spirit. However, just as it has always been, YHWH will accomplish His purposes *through His people*. This is consistent with the way YHWH has always worked in and through His people.

YHWH promises that He will breathe new spiritual life into the House of Ephraim, and that we will 'come up from our graves' in a metaphoric sense.

> **14 I will put My Spirit in you, and you shall live, and I will settle you in your own land. Then you shall know that I, YHWH, have spoken it and performed it," says YHWH.'"**

What this passage gives us is the following sequence of events within the House of Israel (Ephraim):

1. Ephraim is spiritually dead (verse 1);
2. Then there was a noise (verse 7);
3. Then there was a rattling (verse 7);
4. Then the bones (i.e., the leaders) begin coming together, bone to bone (verse 7);
5. Then sinews, flesh and skin (the people, the assemblies, etc.) come upon them (verse 8);
6. Then the breath/spirit (רוח) comes into them;
7. Then they stand upon their feet, an exceedingly great army (a literal nation); and then finally
8. YHWH brings Ephraim back home.

We will talk more about the specifics of the unification process in coming chapters. However, before we can talk about the unification process, first we need to understand the prophecy of the 'Two Sticks' that is spoken about in the second half of Ezekiel 37.

The Two Sticks

In the second half of Ezekiel 37, Ezekiel was told to take two 'sticks' for himself (one for each of the Two Houses of Israel), and then to bring them together as one in his hand.

> *Yehezqel (Ezekiel) 37:15-17*
> *15 Again the word of YHWH came to me, saying,*
> *16a "As for you, son of man, take a stick (עֵץ) for yourself and write on it: 'For Judah and for the children of Israel, his companions.'*
> *16b Then take another stick (עֵץ) and write on it, 'For Joseph, the Stick of Ephraim, and for all the House of Israel, his companions.'*
> *17 Then join them one to another for yourself into one stick (עֵץ), and they will become one in your hand.*

This passage tells us that the two sticks are symbolic of the Two Houses, but why exactly did YHWH choose the word 'stick'? What is so special about this word 'stick' in the Hebrew, that YHWH uses it to represent the Two Houses here?

In the Hebrew, the word 'stick' is the word 'etz' (עֵץ). Strong's Concordance tells us that this word means first and foremost '*tree*' (while the word '*stick*' is actually a secondary [or even a tertiary] derivation).

> OT:6086 `ets (עץ); from OT:6095; a <u>tree</u> (from its firmness); hence, wood (plural sticks).

Since the word etz (עץ) means 'tree,' we should also be able to see that the Two 'Sticks' of Ezekiel 37 are the Two Olive Trees of Revelation 11:3-4.

> *Gilyana (Revelation) 11:3-4*
> *3 "And I will give power to my two witnesses, and they will prophesy one thousand two hundred and sixty days, clothed in sackcloth."*
> *4 These are the two olive trees and the two lampstands standing before the Elohim of the earth.*

If:
1. the Two Houses are the Two Sticks, and
2. if the Two Sticks are the Two Olive Trees, and
3. if the Two Olive Trees are the Two Witnesses,
4. then by extension, the Two Houses, (Ephraim and Judah) are the Two Witnesses.

However, we should also take note of the specific language that is used in this passage, because it will show us something very important. Notice that Ezekiel was told to "<u>take</u> a stick" <u>for himself</u> (and to write on it).

> *Yehezqel (Ezekiel) 37:16a*
> *16a "As for you, son of man, take a stick for yourself and write on it: 'For Judah and for the children of Israel, his companions.'*

Most Pre-Millennial Return Theorists will insist that the term 'son of man' can only refer to Yeshua. However, while Yeshua did sometimes refer to Himself as the "Son of Man," the majority of times the term 'son of man' is used in Scripture, it refers to a human (and not to an immortal being, such as Yeshua). Moreover, in context, it is fairly clear that YHWH commanded the man *Ezekiel* to take this stick (and not Yeshua).

But why did YHWH command the man Ezekiel to *take* a stick? And what does it mean symbolically, that the man Ezekiel would *'take'* a stick (and write on it)?

As we have already seen, the word 'stick' (עץ) in this passage means, 'a tree.'

> *OT:6086 `ets (עץ); from OT:6095; a <u>tree</u> (from its firmness); hence, wood (plural sticks).*

The word עץ, however, basically refers to wood in its natural form (trees, wood, and sticks). The thing that trees, sticks, and other pieces of wood all have in common, then, is their *firmness*. They are not piles of sawdust, or splinters. Rather, they are solid, and cohesive. They have structure, form and *firmness*.

Interestingly, if these Two Olive Trees will be made into one, then Scripture tells us that Yeshua is the Root.

> *Gilyana (Revelation) 22:16*
> *16 "I, Yeshua, have sent My messenger (angel) to testify to you these things in the churches. I am the Root and the Offspring of David, the Bright and Morning Star."*

The Apostle Shaul appears to have been aware of the requirement for Judah and Ephraim to become one Olive Tree when he wrote his epistle to the Romans.

> *Romim (Romans) 11:16-17*
> *16 For if the firstfruit is set-apart, the lump is also set-apart; and if the root is set-apart, so are the branches.*
> *17 And if some of the branches were broken off, and you, being a wild olive tree, were grafted in among them, and with them became a partaker of the root and fatness of the olive tree, 18 do not boast against the branches. But if you do boast, remember that you do not support the Root, but the Root supports you.*

Even back in the first century, the Apostle Shaul knew what Ezekiel 37 foretold: which was that the way to get Judah saved was to mobilize the Ephraimites, and to bring them together as a 'stick' (i.e., a nation); and that it would be *by virtue* of the Ephraimite people coming together as a nation under Torah that Judah would ultimately be provoked to jealousy (and to salvation).

> *Romim (Romans) 11:11-15*
> *11 I say then, have they stumbled that they should fall? Certainly not! But through their fall, to provoke them to jealousy, salvation has come to the Gentiles.*
> *12 Now if their fall is riches for the world, and their failure riches for the Gentiles (i.e., Ephraimites), how much more their fullness!*

> **13 For I speak to you Gentiles; inasmuch as I am an apostle to the Gentiles, I magnify my ministry, 14 if by any means I may provoke to jealousy those who are my flesh and save some of them.**
> **15 For if their being cast away is the reconciling of the world, what will their acceptance be but life from the dead?**

It was not by making 'Christians' out of 'gentiles' that Shaul would see the Jewish people accept Yeshua as their long-awaited Messiah. Rather, it was when the Jewish people saw that Yeshua was the *reason* the Ephraimite people voluntarily submitted to the whole of the Torah that Judah would be unable to escape the conclusion that Yeshua really is their Messiah.

What is so exciting, then, is that while Shaul labored so long and so hard to help bring Ephraim back together as a literal nation back in the first century, the actual reformation of the Stick (or the Nation) of Ephraim is prophesied to take place in our day. If we do not see it take place ourselves, then our children surely will.

But does Scripture give us any clues as to *how* Ephraim will be reformed as a nation? If we look at Ezekiel 37, can we see *how* this will happen?

Notice that in Ezekiel 37, first Ezekiel *'takes'* a Stick for Judah (and writes on it), and then Ezekiel *'takes'* a Stick for Joseph (and writes on it). The specific language is the same for both Houses; and what this should tell us is that the Stick of Ephraim will be brought together in *exactly the same way* that the Stick of Judah was brought together.

What is so fascinating about Ezekiel 37, then, is that by seeing what happened to Judah, we can also know pretty much what will happen with Ephraim.

1. If the Stick of Judah mentioned in Ezekiel 37 is the Nation of Israel in the Middle East; and
2. If the Two Sticks are the Two Houses (as Ezekiel 37 says); and
3. If Ezekiel was a human being,
4. Then Ezekiel 37 tells us that
5. The Stick of Ephraim will be brought together through inspired human effort (just as the Stick of Judah was); and that
6. The Two Houses will *also* be brought back together through inspired human effort. Why?

In 1896, a man named Theodore Herzl wrote a booklet called *Der Judenstadt* (the Jewish State). This booklet proposed that the only real solution to Christian anti-Semitism was for the Jewish people to reclaim their ancient homeland (centered about Mount Zion).

As with Martin Luther's 95 *Theses*, the idea of a Jewish State had been proposed before; but thanks to YHWH, in 1896 it was an idea whose time had finally come. Soon after *Der Judenstadt* was published, the Jewish community began pressing for a Jewish State, and the Zionist Movement was born. Fifty-two years and a Holocaust later, it finally became a reality.

While Zionism is not synonymous with Judaism, the Zionist Movement cannot really be considered a secular movement. Just the fact that Zionism proposed that the Jewish people should center themselves about Mount Zion makes it scripturally related. Notice also how this is related to the idea that Ezekiel was not just any old (secular) human being, but a priest.

Yehezqel (Ezekiel) 1:3
3 The word of YHWH came expressly to Ezekiel the priest, the son of Buzi, in the land of the Chaldeans by the River Chebar; and the hand of YHWH was upon him there.

While it may be true that Zionism is only a populist least-common-religious-denominator among the Jewish people, it was nonetheless Zionism that made the State of Israel a reality. It was this common Jewish desire to escape Christian persecution, as well as Judah's deep-seated yearning to reconnect with his ancient Middle Eastern homeland that ultimately paved the way for the establishment of modern Israeli religious institutions (such as the Sanhedrin).

Much as Constitutionalism is fueled by Pre-Millennialist American Christian sentiment, Zionism is fueled by populist Jewish religious sentiment. We will talk later in this book about how a corresponding Ephraimite least-common-religious-denominator will be used to draw the Ephraimite people back to the Land of Israel, but first, let us notice something important.

If we look at the plain and simple meaning of the Text, Ezekiel was not told just to sit around and wait to be *handed* a stick. He was also not told that Yeshua would take him back to the Land of Israel in the clouds. Rather, Ezekiel was told to take a stick *for himself*, and identify it as belonging to the House of Judah (by writing on it). And, if we look at the history, this is a perfect picture of what the Jewish people did: they formed themselves into a nation, thereby taking a stick *for themselves*, and then they identified it as belonging to Judah (just as the Prophet Ezekiel foretold).

Now, if we Ephraimites can understand that Yeshua is not going to bring us back to the Land of Israel in a cloud (wind whipping through our hair, sunglasses on, theme music playing), then we should also be able to see that Ezekiel 37 requires Ephraim to come back to the Land in the same way that Judah came back to the Land: That is, we must take a stick (i.e., a nation) *for ourselves*, and then identify it as belonging to Ephraim. That is to say, we must establish a nation *for ourselves*.

> **Yehezqel (Ezekiel) 37:15-17**
> **15 Again the word of YHWH came to me, saying,**
> **16a "As for you, son of man, take a stick for yourself and write on it: 'For Judah and for the children of Israel, his companions.'**
> **16b Then take another stick and write on it, 'For Joseph, the Stick of Ephraim, and for all the House of Israel, his companions.'**
> **17 Then join them one to another for yourself into one stick, and they will become one in your hand.**

Just as Judah had to make a nation for himself, so too must Ephraim make a nation for himself. To believe anything else is essentially to suggest that Ezekiel 37 will not come to pass just exactly as it is written (which is essentially to suggest that Ezekiel 37 is not inspired, which is essentially to call YHWH a liar).

Pre-Millennialism suggests that Ezekiel *is* a liar: It tells us that it would be heretical for us to make a nation for ourselves, even though prophecy requires it. Further, it suggests that it is wrong to be used to fulfill Prophecy.

Pre-Millennial Return Theory argues that it *is* wrong (and altogether presumptuous) for any human being to believe that they can be used to fulfill prophecy. As if to prove their point, they remind us (for example) that it was YHWH (and not any man) who brought our forefathers out of Egypt.

> **Yirmeyahu (Jeremiah) 32:21-22**
> **21 "You have brought Your people Israel out of the land of Egypt with signs and wonders, with a strong hand and an outstretched arm, and with great terror;**
> **22 You have given them this land, of which You swore to their fathers to give them — "a land flowing with milk and honey."**

The post-millennialist knows that it was YHWH who brought the children of Israel out of Egypt. However, the post-millennialist also knows that YHWH *used* *Moshe* to bring them out. Further, the post-millennialist points out that while it was YHWH who gave the Land of Israel to His people, He nonetheless *used* Yehoshua (Joshua) to *lead* His people to *take* the Land.

To drive the point home, the post-millennialist asks us to be aware of who smote Amalek.

> **Shemote (Exodus) 17:14**
> **14 Then YHWH said to Moshe, "Write this for a memorial in the book and recount it in the hearing of Yehoshua (Joshua), that I will utterly blot out the remembrance of Amalek from under heaven."**

YHWH plainly said that He would smite Amalek; and yet YHWH commanded Israel to *perform* that smiting.

> **Devarim (Deuteronomy) 25:17-19**
> **17 "Remember what Amalek did to you on the way as you were coming out of Egypt, 18 how he met you on the way and attacked your rear ranks, all the stragglers at your rear, when you were tired and weary; and he did not fear Elohim.**
> **19 Therefore it shall be, when YHWH your Elohim has given you rest from your enemies all around, in the land which YHWH your Elohim is giving you to possess as an inheritance, that you will blot out the remembrance of Amalek from under heaven. You shall not forget.**

It was YHWH who smote Amalek; and yet YHWH *used* Israel to smite Amalek, just like He *used* Moshe to draw Israel out of Egypt (just as He *used* Yehoshua ben Nun to lead the conquest of the Land, and just as the children of Israel had to *take* the Land in the first place). This is because while nothing happens by our own power and strength, YHWH typically works in (and through) His people. Can we see the connection?

Therefore, let us acknowledge that it was YHWH's Spirit that led the Jewish Zionist Movement to fulfill Ezekiel 37. It was by only the leading and guiding of YHWH's Spirit that Judah ever 'took' a stick for himself. Therefore, will it not *also* be by the leading and guiding of YHWH's Spirit that Ephraim will take a stick for himself? Is this not what Ezekiel 37 says?

The pre-millennialists refuse to acknowledge any of this. Instead, they cling to their theory about Yeshua returning at the start of the Millennium, because the thought of Yeshua doing all the work just seems easier.

Ironically, when faced with the fact that Scripture requires Ephraim to *work* to rebuild his nation, the pre-millennialist generally becomes angry. He hates the thought that he might actually have to work to go back home to the Land. The thought of having to earn his reward seems loathsome to him.

But let us ask ourselves, what kind of *spirit* is it that claims to be dead to the flesh, and which yet finds the thought of having to support Yeshua's priesthood to be *hateful* (and not joyful)? What kind of spirit *says* it wants to lay down its life for Yeshua, and yet hates the thought of working to build Yeshua's kingdom? Is it the Set-apart Spirit that says these things?

If these thoughts seem strange, consider that in Ezekiel 36, YHWH told Ephraim that first He would give him a new spirit, and then bring him back to His Land. Then, *after* Ephraim is brought back to the Land, then YHWH will give Ephraim so much of His Spirit that Ephraim will even begin to loathe himself.

> ***Yehezqel (Ezekiel) 36:31-32***
> ***31 Then** you will remember your evil ways and your deeds that were not good; and you will loathe yourselves in your own sight, for your iniquities and your abominations.*
> ***32** Not for your sake do I do this," says YHWH Elohim, "let it be known to you. Be ashamed and confounded for your own ways, O House of Israel!"*

Now, if Ephraim first comes back to the Land, and *then* loathes himself for his *own* ways, that would seem to suggest that the House of Israel will **not** come back to the Land in a completely pure state. Rather, it will only be *after* his return that he is given true purity.

However, this raises the question, "Why would the House of Israel even want to come back to the Land, if it is not already pure? Is it not a desire for purity that makes one want to return to the Land to begin with? And if the House of Israel is not *already* completely pure, then why would it *want* to come back?"

The answer is that Ephraim has never really been pure. While YHWH says He will give him a desire for *more* purity, his purity has pretty-much always been relative; and in fact, the object of his numerous migrations over the past 2730 years has never really been true purity, but subjective purity. That is to say, he has not really sought what is right in YHWH's eyes, but in his own.

As we will discuss in *Migrations: the Lost Ten Tribes,* when the main prophetic body of the House of Israel migrated from the Old World to the New, Ephraim was indeed seeking a form of purity. Religious Protestants left the Old World to make a new and better life for their children; and yet it was the lawless Christian ideal (and not a Torah-obedient one) that they sought.

Ephraim still desires this better life. However, with the continuing deterioration of Christian social and cultural values in the United States (as well as in other Western countries), and with literal witchcraft (i.e. *Harry Potter,* 'Earth Day,' etcetera) being taught to America's children, how long will it be before Ephraim finds his Judeo-Christian social and cultural values even more unwelcome than they already are?

Judeo-Christian beliefs are illegal in many countries, and in today's America, it is now considered unlawful to restrict marriage to men and women only. Many other traditional 'Christian' values are already classified as 'hate crimes' in America's courts; and the trend against Judeo-Christian values is generally getting worse.

Since the days of World War Two, American society has been utterly transformed. In the 1960's the Ten Commandments were taken out of the public schools. American society in general has departed from the Judeo-Christian way of life, and Judeo-Christian belief is now openly ridiculed in all walks of life. Therefore, what aspects of Torah life can we expect to see marginalized and/or criminalized as America's Judeo-Christian minority continues to shrink, while the *Harry Potter* Generation comes of voting age?

If YHWH wants to make Ephraim earnestly desire to return to the Land of Israel, all He really has to do is to allow the American political and cultural scene to continue to deteriorate. The way things are going, America will soon enough criminalize Judeo-Christian social and cultural values.

But aside from speculating on the anti-religious and cultural pressures that will probably be placed on true believers in the coming decades, we should also note that Prophecy speaks of a series of several wars with the Muslim people.

With Islamic oil money going to support terrorist activism internationally, and with some eleven million Muslims now living in the United States, what kind of terrorism does America have to fear on her own shores in the coming years? What kind of 'fifth column' action can she expect from her own citizens?

Islam is one of the fastest-growing religions in the world. There are now more than one billion Muslims: and the number is growing rapidly.

While originally founded as a Judeo-Christian nation, the United States now has Islamic senators and congressmen. At the time of this writing there is even an Islamic presidential candidate. How does this play into prophecy?

Before we talk about how to reform the Ephraimite nation (and thus move Judah to jealousy, and bring about the Ingathering) let us turn for a moment and explore what Scripture has to tell us about the coming wars with Islam. Then let us also consider the effects of the coming terrorism on American soil.

The Millennial Land

In *Nazarene Israel*, we explained how the Christian people are the prophetic (and perhaps also the literal) descendants of the Lost Ten Tribes of Israel. Even though there has been a lot of grafting in and out (i.e., genetic drift) over time, the Protestant Christian people remain the only group on earth which fulfills all of the prophecies given over the Lost Ten Tribes.

Yeshua tells us that many will come from east and west, and sit down with Avraham, Yitzhak and Ya'akov (Abraham, Isaac and Jacob) in the kingdom of heaven.

> **Mattai (Matthew) 8:11**
> **11 And I say to you that many will come from east and west, and sit down with Avraham, Yitzhak and Ya'akov in the kingdom of heaven.**

As we explain in *Nazarene Israel*, one of the reasons that YHWH will call believers from both east and west is that YHWH loves all of mankind. He does not really care about our racial makeup; but about our spirit. He wants *all* of fallen Adam's children to come to the knowledge of the truth; and that is why whosoever shall believe on His Son (to the point of obeying Torah) shall be saved. However, while we can look forward to the Millennial Kingdom being filled with people from every tribe, tongue and ethnic background, this does not mean that all of the nations of earth have been given the same roles to play, in prophecy.

As we discuss in *Nazarene Israel* (and as we will also discuss in *Migrations: The Lost Ten Tribes*), when the Ephraimites migrated northward and westward (by three separate migration routes) to what would later become Protestant northwestern Europe, the tribes as prophetic bodies each ended up aligned more-or-less with what later became the countries (or ethnic groups) of Europe, and/or their associated empires.

For example, the Tribe of Dan eventually became intermixed and in-grafted into the Germanic people. This is why there are names such as the *Dan*-ube River, *Dan*-mark (Denmark), and Gutenberg (Gut-dan-berg) in the areas settled by the ethnic Germans.

For another example, Holland is probably populated with the descendants of Zebulon, whose children were prophesied to dwell by the haven of the sea, and to become a haven for ships (Genesis 49:13).

As we discuss in *Nazarene Israel*, England is the modern-day prophetic representative of Manasseh, as the name Manasseh means, "He shall forget his toil, and (forget) his father's house." This is why the Industrial Revolution first came about in Britain: it was so the Manassites would forget their toil (due to the benefits of industrialization), and also forget their Father's House (through such replacement-theologies as the heretical 'British Israel' thesis).

America, then, is the prophetic representative of the Tribe of Ephraim, which serves as the lead tribe in representing the House of Ephraim. America was England's 'younger brother,' and became greater than the older (Genesis 48:19); and both the ex-British Empire and the Americans have become like a teeming multitude of fishes in the earth (Genesis 48:16).

While the tribal affiliations were originally pure, they are all-scrambled-up today, particularly for those who live in the New World. Many people therefore concern themselves with questions as to 'which tribe they might belong to,' but as we will explain elsewhere, such questions are not really important. Ezekiel 47-48 tells us that when the Ephraimites come back to the Land (after a victorious war with Islam), tribal affiliations will be re-assigned based upon the geographical *location* into which one settles (rather than upon any question of race, ethnicity, or genetic heritage).

And yet, these finer points of Scripture are generally ignored by the Muslims, who consider that the Jews and the Christians are really just two halves of the same whole (i.e., 'people of the Book'). This is one reason why the Islamic nations call America the 'Great Satan,' and Israel the 'Little Satan.' This is also why the Islamic war-cry is, "First the Saturday people, (and) then the Sunday people:" they see scant little difference between Christians and Jews.

Islamic animosity towards the Jews and the Christians is not really a secret. Islamic law dictates that every human being must convert to Islam, or else be put to death as an 'infidel.' This militant theology is the cause of the repeated Muslim attacks on Israel and against the United States, in such incidents as the 9-1-1 Tragedy, the Achille Lauro, the bombing of the U.S.S. Cole, the terrorist attack in the 1972 Munich Olympic Games, and many, many more.

The truth is that Islam has already essentially declared war on both Israel and America, and the only thing restraining them from attacking us at this time is their lack of adequate means. However, Islamic nuclear scientists are working diligently to close this gap.

But who are the Muslim people? Where do they come from? And why do they seem so implacably hostile towards both Jews and Christians alike?

We have already seen that the Book of Genesis is prophetic, in that the events listed in Genesis recur throughout Scripture (and history). Notice, then, that Genesis Sixteen tells us that when Sarah was not able to bear children unto Avraham, she asked Avraham to impregnate her maidservant Hagar, so that maybe she (Sarah) would obtain children by her (Hagar). Avraham did so, but then, when Hagar conceived, she began to despise Sarah (here called *Sarai*).

> **B'reisheet (Genesis) 16:1-4**
> **16:1 Now Sarai, Avram's wife, had borne him no children. And she had an Egyptian maidservant whose name was Hagar.**
> **2 So Sarai said to Avram, "See now, YHWH has restrained me from bearing children. Please, go in to my maid; perhaps I shall obtain children by her." And Avram heeded the voice of Sarai.**
> **3 Then Sarai, Avram's wife, took Hagar her maid, the Egyptian, and gave her to her husband Avram to be his wife, after Avram had dwelt ten years in the land of Canaan.**
> **4 So he went in to Hagar, and she conceived. And when she saw that she had conceived, her mistress (Sarah) became despised in her eyes.**

But what should we learn from this? Why would it be important to know that Hagar *despised* Sarah (Sarai)?

As we also saw in *Nazarene Israel*, Genesis One tells us that living beings reproduce after their own *kinds*.

> **B'reisheet (Genesis) 1:24**
> **24 Then Elohim said, "Let the earth bring forth the living creature according to its kind: cattle and creeping thing and beast of the earth, each according to its kind"; and it was so.**

Since living beings reproduce after their own *kinds*, it should follow that Hagar's descendants would tend to despise Sarah's children (i.e., the Jews and the Christians/Ephraimites). This is in fact what we do see.

As another witness, Scripture also tells us that Hagar's son was named Ishmael; and that he scoffed at the great festival that Avraham threw, in honor of the weaning of Sarah's son Yitzhak (Isaac).

> **B'reisheet (Genesis) 21:8-9**
> **8 So the child (Yitzhak) grew and was weaned. And Avraham made a great feast on the same day that Yitzhak was weaned.**
> **9 And Sarah saw the son of Hagar the Egyptian, whom she had borne to Avraham, scoffing.**

But how do we know that the Muslim peoples are really the Ishmaelites? Well, for one thing, the Muslims *claim* to descend from Ishmael; and according to Scripture, self-identification with a given religious belief set is what actually determines one's Scriptural nationality.

[Let us note that when the Assyrians took the Ephraimites out of the Land, the next generations of Ephraimites no longer self-identified as Ephraimites. Instead, they began self-identifying as Assyrians, and so they became Assyrians (i.e., 'gentiles'). Then, as the dispersed Ephraimites no longer lived in the Land, no longer spoke Hebrew and no longer kept the Torah, the Jewish rabbis rightly ruled that they could no longer be called Ephraimites; but that they should now be called 'gentiles,' seeing as they no longer behaved anything like YHWH's covenant people Israel.]

Other passages confirm that the Islamic people really do descend from Ishmael. For example, one more-or-less direct link is how Esau married one of Ishmael's daughters, named Mahalath (also called Basemath in Genesis 36:4).

> *B'reisheet (Genesis) 28:8-9*
> *8 Also Esau saw that the daughters of Canaan did not please his father Yitzhak.*
> *9 So Esau went to Ishmael and took Mahalath the daughter of Ishmael, Avraham's son, the sister of Nebajoth, to be his wife in addition to the wives he had.*

We are also told that Esau is Edom, and Edom's historical territorial homeland lies just east of the present-day Land of Israel, in what is now modern-day (Islamic) Jordan.

> *B'reisheet (Genesis) 36:1-4*
> *36:1 Now this is the genealogy of Esau, who is Edom.*

> *2 Esau took his wives from the daughters of Canaan: Adah the daughter of Elon the Hittite; Aholibamah the daughter of Anah, the daughter of Zibeon the Hivite;*
> *3 and Basemath (Mahalath), Ishmael's daughter, sister of Nebajoth.*

Scripture tells us that the Ishmaelites are not the Covenant People, in that the Promise was to come through Ya'akov (Jacob). However, Elohim did give Ishmael blessings of great physical multiplicity.

> *B'reisheet (Genesis) 17:19-21*
> *19 Then Elohim said: "No! Sarah your wife shall bear you a son, and you shall call his name Yitzhak (Isaac). I will establish My covenant with him for an everlasting covenant, and with his descendants after him.*
> *20 And as for Ishmael, I have heard you. Behold, I have blessed him, and will make him fruitful, and will multiply him exceedingly. He shall beget twelve princes, and I will make him a great nation.*
> *21 But My covenant I will establish with Yitzhak (Isaac), whom Sarah shall bear to you at this set time next year."*

Verse 20 tells us that Ishmael would beget twelve princes, and there are twelve Arabic (Ishmaeli) nations in which Islamic law is woven into the fabric of society. These are Egypt, Jordan, Turkey, Saudi Arabia, Oman, Iran, Iraq, the United Arab Emirates, and etcetera.

However, if we saw that Ishmael, Esau and Edom can all be equated with Islam, then we should also take special notice that Esau was a hunter.

> **B'reisheet (Genesis) 25:27**
> **27 So the boys grew. And Esau was a skillful hunter, a man of the field; but Ya'akov was a complete man, dwelling in tents.**

Jeremiah 31, then, tells us that America is only a temporary resting stop for the House of Ephraim, before he is brought back to the Land.

> **Yirmeyahu (Jeremiah) 31:2**
> **2 Thus says YHWH:**
> **"The people who survived the sword found favor in the wilderness — Israel, when I went to give him rest."**

But if America is only a temporary resting stop (i.e., the place where Ephraim finally comes to his senses), Jeremiah 16 tells us that first YHWH would send for many *fishermen*, to bring the Ephraimites back home; and then (when that did not work) YHWH would send for many *hunters* (to *drive* His people back home).

> **Yirmeyahu (Jeremiah) 16:16-19**
> **16 "Behold, I will send for many fishermen," says YHWH, "and they shall fish them; and afterward I will send for many hunters, and they shall hunt them from every mountain and every hill, and out of the holes of the rocks.**

And, if Esau is a *hunter*, Scripture also tells us that Ishmael (i.e., the Muslim people) was an *archer*.

> **B'reisheet (Genesis) 21:20**
> **20 So Elohim was with the lad (Ishmael); and he grew and dwelt in the wilderness, and became an archer.**

If the fishermen are perhaps the Nazarenes, then the *hunters* are the Islamic peoples (Ishmael/Islam), who are now in the process of developing nuclear and chemical weapons. This is a problem, in that we saw how these *archers* are prophesied to "bitterly grieve" both America and the ex-British Empire (who are Ephraim and Manasseh, respectively).

> **B'reisheet (Genesis) 49:22-24**
> **22 "Joseph is a fruitful bough, a fruitful bough by a well; his branches run over the wall.**
> **23 The archers have bitterly grieved him, shot at him and hated him.**
> **24 But his bow remained in strength, and the arms of his hands were made strong by the hands of the Mighty One of Ya'akov. From there (i.e., Joseph) is the Shepherd, the Stone of Israel.**

The Islamic designs on the Judeo-Christian world are no real surprise. If we just pay close attention to the headlines from month to month, the Islamic plans to attack Israel, America and England (followed by the ex-British Empire countries of Australia and New Zealand) are plain as day. Therefore, are the days that the archers will grieve Joseph not fast approaching?

One comfort is that post-millennial theory gives us a realistic scenario by which the Land of Israel might be expanded to become the Millennial Land.

The present-day Land of Israel is actually quite small; perhaps the same size as New Jersey. However, Scripture Prophecy speaks of an expanded Millennial Land stretching from the River of Egypt to the River Euphrates.

> **B'reisheet (Genesis) 15:18**
> **18 On the same day YHWH made a covenant with Avram, saying:**
> **"To your descendants I have given this land, from the river of Egypt to the great river, the River Euphrates...."**

Scholars do not agree as to the exact boundaries and dimensions of the Millennial Land. However, it does seem that the boundaries of the Millennial Land are prophetically related to Avraham's travels.

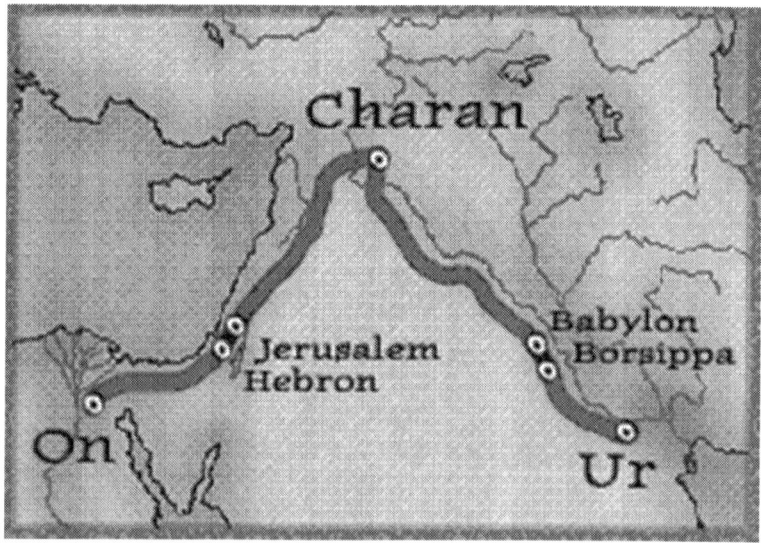

Avraham began his life as Avram, in Ur of the Kasdim (Chaldees). Ur lies to the east of the land of Israel, in what is now modern-day Iraq. This is closer to the mouth of the Euphrates River (near the Persian Gulf).

> **B'reisheet (Genesis) 11:31**
> **31 And Terah took his son Avram and his grandson Lot, the son of Haran, and his daughter-in-law Sarai, his son Avram's wife, and they went out with them from Ur of the Chaldeans to go to the land of Canaan; and they came to Haran and dwelt there.**

Interestingly, this passage tells us that Haran (which lies on the Euphrates River) is actually *part* of the land of Canaan. But what does this mean?

We should also note that it was in Haran (in modern-day Syria) that YHWH first spoke to Avraham, telling him to leave his home and his father's house, to go to a land that YHWH would show him. And so it was that, leaving Haran, Avraham went first to Shechem.

> **B'reisheet (Genesis) 12:1-9**
> **12:1 Now YHWH had said to Avram: "Get out of your country, from your family and from your father's house, to a land that I will show you.**
> **2 I will make you a great nation. I will bless you and make your name great; and you shall be a blessing.**
> **3 I will bless those who bless you, and I will curse him who curses you; and in you all the families of the earth shall be blessed."**

> *4 So Avram departed as YHWH had spoken to him, and Lot went with him. And Avram was seventy-five years old when he departed from Haran.*
> *5 Then Avram took Sarai his wife and Lot his brother's son, and all their possessions that they had gathered, and the people whom they had acquired in Haran, and they departed to go to the land of Canaan. So they came to the land of Canaan.*
> *6 Avram passed through the land to the place of Shechem, as far as the terebinth tree of Moreh. And the Canaanites were then in the land.*

YHWH first appeared to Avraham in Shechem, telling him that his descendants would inherit all the Land of Canaan. Thus it was only *after* Avraham had stepped out in faith that YHWH bestowed His blessings upon him. (For more information as to why it was actually Yeshua who appeared to Avraham, please see 'Manifestation of Elohim,' at www.nazareneisrael.org.)

> *7 Then YHWH appeared to Avram and said, "To your descendants I will give this land." And there he built an altar to YHWH, who had appeared to him.*
> *8 And he moved from there to the mountain east of Bethel, and he pitched his tent with Bethel on the west and Ai on the east; there he built an altar to YHWH and called on the name of YHWH.*
> *9 So Avram journeyed, going on still toward the South.*

Avraham traveled south, and dwelt in Hevron (Hebron). While there, YHWH appeared to Avraham in a vision, and told him that it had been He who had first brought him out of Ur of the Kasdim (Chaldees).

> **B'reisheet (Genesis) 15:7**
> **7 Then He said to him, "I am YHWH, who brought you out of Ur of the Chaldeans, to give you this land to inherit it."**

YHWH told Avraham that his descendants would inherit all of the land from the Euphrates River, to the River of Egypt, and even identified the ten nations whom Israel would ideally displace. If we study into these nations a little bit, it will show us something very instructive about the borders of the Millennial Land.

> **B'reisheet (Genesis) 15:19-21**
> **18 On the same day YHWH made a covenant with Avram, saying:**
> **"To your descendants I have given this land, from the river of Egypt to the great river, the River Euphrates:**
> **19 the Kenites, the Kenezzites, the Kadmonites,**
> **20 the Hittites, the Perizzites, the Rephaim,**
> **21 the Amorites, the Canaanites, the Girgashites, and the Jebusites."**

We should note that when YHWH later brought the children of Israel out of Egypt and into the Land of Canaan (under Joshua), they were told to displace only *seven* nations; and some of the names are different.

> Devarim (Deuteronomy) 7:1-5
> "When YHWH your Elohim brings you into the land which you go to possess, and has cast out many nations before you, the Hittites and the Girgashites and the Amorites and the Canaanites and the Perizzites and the Hivites and the Jebusites, seven nations greater and mightier than you...."

The Jewish commentators identify Rephaim with the Hivites, but the Kenites, the Kenezzites and the Kadmonites are missing from this second list.

Who are the missing three nations that Israel did not displace at the time of the conquest of the Land of Canaan, but who will eventually be displaced for the Millennial Land? Opinions differ, but many scholars identify the Kenites, Kenezzites and the Kadmonites with Edom, Moab and Ammon (of modern-day Jordan). This would make perfect sense, in that Israel is prophesied to conquer (and perhaps annex) these lands in the reasonably near future (see below).

For example, Isaiah speaks about how America and Israel will conquer both the Gaza Strip, and Jordan.

> Yeshayahu (Isaiah) 11:14
> 14 But they (Joseph and Judah) shall fly down upon the shoulder of the Philistines toward the west (i.e., Gaza). Together they shall plunder the people of the East (i.e., Jordan). They shall lay their hand on Edom (in Jordan) and Moab (in Jordan), and the people of Ammon (in Jordan) shall obey them.

Isaiah also tells us that YHWH will destroy the tongue of the Sea of Egypt, which is probably a reference to the Nile River Delta; and that there will be a highway set up between Egypt and Assyria, so that Egypt, Assyria and the Land of Israel will all become one.

> *Yeshayahu (Isaiah) 11:15-16*
> *15 YHWH will utterly destroy the tongue of the Sea of Egypt (possibly the Nile River Delta). With His mighty wind He will shake His fist over the River, and strike it in the seven streams, and make men cross over dryshod.*
> *16 There will be a highway for the remnant of His people who will be left from Assyria, as it was for Israel in the day that he came up from the land of Egypt.*

Most rabbinical commentators suggest that the term "river of Egypt" (as used in Genesis 15:18) is not actually a reference to the Nile River, but rather a reference to the 'Brook of Egypt,' which formed part of the ideal southwestern border of the Land of Israel at the time of its original conquest (under Joshua).

> *Bemidbar (Numbers) 34:5*
> *5 the border shall turn from Azmon to the Brook of Egypt, and it shall end at the Sea.*

This 'Brook of Egypt' is today identified as the Wadi El-Aris, which bisects the Sinai Peninsula (running north-south through it).

There are problems with the rabbinical view. We have already seen that Isaiah 11:15 (above) tells us that YHWH will strike the River of Egypt in its seven streams. This cannot possibly be the Wadi El-Aris, because the Wadi El-Aris does not have seven streams (nor does it always run with water).

Further, Isaiah Nineteen gives us a second witness that the Millennial Land will one day extend all of the way from Assyria unto the Land of Egypt (not stopping at the Wadi El-Aris).

> *Yeshayahu (Isaiah) 19:18-25*
> *18 In that day five cities in the land of Egypt will speak the language of Canaan and swear by YHWH of hosts; one will be called the City of Destruction.*
> *19 In that day there will be an altar to YHWH in the midst of the land of Egypt, and a pillar to YHWH at its border.*
> *20 And it will be for a sign and for a witness to YHWH of hosts in the land of Egypt; for they will cry to YHWH because of the oppressors, and He will send them a Savior and a Mighty One, and He will deliver them.*
> *21 Then YHWH will be known to Egypt, and the Egyptians will know YHWH in that day, and will make sacrifice and offering. Yes, they will make a vow to YHWH and perform it.*
> *22 And YHWH will strike Egypt, He will strike and heal it; they will return to YHWH, and He will be entreated by them and heal them.*

> *23 In that day there will be a highway from Egypt to Assyria, and the Assyrian will come into Egypt and the Egyptian into Assyria, and the Egyptians will serve with the Assyrians.*
> *24 In that day Israel will be one of three with Egypt and Assyria — a blessing in the midst of the land,*
> *25 whom YHWH of hosts shall bless, saying, "Blessed is Egypt My people, and Assyria the work of My hands, and Israel My inheritance."*

But if we can see that the Land of Israel will one day be greatly expanded, then the question remains, *how* will these lands ultimately become annexed by the present day State of Israel? The answer probably lies in the fact that Scripture calls for the United States and Israel to fight together against a common Islamic foe.

We have already seen how Prophecy calls for the Muslims to attack the descendants of the House of Joseph (i.e., America, and possibly Britain, and others).

> *B'reisheet (Genesis) 49:22-24*
> *22 "Joseph is a fruitful bough, a fruitful bough by a well; his branches run over the wall.*
> *23 The archers have bitterly grieved him, shot at him and hated him.*
> *24 But his bow remained in strength, and the arms of his hands were made strong by the hands of the Mighty One of Ya'akov. From there (i.e., Joseph) is the Shepherd, the Stone of Israel.*

Zechariah tells us that Judah and Joseph (essentially Israel and America, and possibly Great Britain and/or elements of the old British Empire) will fight together (and win) against a common Muslim foe.

> *Zechariah 10:5-10*
> *5 They (Judah and Ephraim) shall be like mighty men, who tread down their enemies in the mire of the streets in the battle. They shall fight because YHWH is <u>with</u> them, and the riders on horses shall be put to shame.*
> *6 "I will strengthen the House of Judah, and I will save the House of Joseph. I will bring them back because I have mercy on them. They shall be as though I had not cast them aside, for I am YHWH their Elohim, and I will hear them.*
> *7 Those of Ephraim shall be like a mighty man, and their heart shall rejoice as if with wine. Yes, their children shall see it and be glad; their heart shall rejoice in YHWH.*
> *8 I will whistle for them and gather them, for I will redeem them; and they shall increase as they once increased.*
> *9 "I will sow them among the peoples, And they shall remember Me in far countries. They shall live, together with their children, and they shall return.*
> *10 I will also bring them back from the land of Egypt, and gather them from Assyria. I will bring them into the land of Gilead and Lebanon until no more room is found for them.*

Verse 10 tells us that the Ephraimites will be brought into Gilead (which is in northwestern Jordan, and possibly also southern Syria) and into Lebanon, until no more room is found for them. This alone speaks of an influx of millions of people.

We should ask ourselves: where will the people who are presently occupying Lebanon and Gilead go? Assuming we are talking about displacing *all* of the residents of those countries, what kind of an outrage will those nations need to commit before the (basically pacifistic and forgiving) Jewish and American peoples encourage their governments to commit what amounts essentially either to ethnic supplantation, or genocide?

To answer this question, let us take a look at some more prophecies. As we have already seen, Isaiah speaks of a war in which Israel and America will fight together, to conquer a common Islamic foe in the Gaza Strip, and in Jordan.

> *Yeshayahu (Isaiah) 11:14-16*
> *14 But they shall fly down upon the shoulder of the Philistines toward the west (i.e., Gaza). Together they shall plunder the people of the East (i.e., Jordan). They shall lay their hand on Edom (in Jordan) and Moab (in Jordan), and the people of Ammon (in Jordan) shall obey them.*
> *15 YHWH will utterly destroy the tongue of the Sea of Egypt (possibly the Nile River Delta). With His mighty wind He will shake His fist over the River, and strike it in the seven streams, and make men cross over dryshod.*

16 There will be a highway for the remnant of His people who will be left from Assyria, as it was for Israel in the day that he came up from the land of Egypt.

It is well-known in intelligence circles that while Jordan pretends to be militarily neutral, in truth, Jordan serves as a quiet supply conduit for Saudi arms, ammunition and explosives. Not only that, but it also provides a safe haven and training grounds for more than one Islamic terror group.

Remembering that Zechariah and Isaiah prophesy the conquest of Lebanon, Jordan, Egypt, and the Gaza Strip, and given the fact that the Islamic world has been promising for years to attack America and the West with nuclear weapons, how difficult is it to believe that the fulfillment of the prophecies in Isaiah and Zechariah will involve an Islamic attack on the U.S.?

Remembering the public furor over the 9-1-1 incident, what kind of response might one expect from America if she were attacked with nuclear weapons? And if it were discovered that these nuclear attacks were staged from Muslim facilities in Jordan, Lebanon and Egypt, how soon would the average voter demand that his government do whatever is necessary to annex the offending countries to Israel, so that no further Islamic nuclear attacks could ever again arise from these countries?

We do not know if our scenario is the one that YHWH will ultimately use to expand the Millennial Land or not: it is just one plausible scenario that seems to fit with all of the prophecies, as well as with the daily news.

However, given the fact that the Muslim world *promises* to attack the United States with weapons of mass destruction, and given the fact that the Islamic world is working hard to accomplish this goal, how realistic is an Islamic nuclear attack on the United States within the next twenty or thirty years? And when this nuclear attack finally takes place, how reasonable is it that the American people would support annexation of all of the offending territories to the State of Israel?

If these things seem plausible (particularly in light of the fact that Prophecy predicts them), then we should note that the first thing any country needs when it annexes new lands, is settlers. Without settlers, newly won lands soon revert to enemy control. But then, from where will these settlers come? That is, who would want to relocate to the Land of Israel?

Clearly, it is the Ephraimites who would want to go back to the Land of Israel.

Remembering that Ezekiel 36 tells us that Ephraim will not return to the Land in a perfectly pure state, we cannot assume that the Ingathering will consist entirely of doctrinally-correct Nazarene Israelites from the Stick of Ephraim. There will be a Stick of Ephraim, and there will be some doctrinally-correct settlers, to be sure, but there will *also* be a 'House of Israel,' his companions.

> *Yehezqel (Ezekiel) 37:16b-17*
> *16b Then take another stick and write on it, 'For Joseph, the Stick of Ephraim, and for all the House of Israel, his companions.'*
> *17 Then join them one to another for yourself into one stick, and they will become one in your hand.*

Who is this "House of Israel" but the Christian Church, running the full gamut all the way from the replacement theological Catholic Church of Rome to the Messianic organizations? No Catholic, Protestant or Messianic organization keeps the full Torah; and these will accompany the Stick of Ephraim back home to the Land of Israel.

This is also why the House of Israel will loathe itself for its iniquities, and its abominations, is that it has taught something less than the full Torah.

> *Yehezqel (Ezekiel) 36:31-32*
> *31 __Then__ you will remember your evil ways and your deeds that were not good; and you will loathe yourselves in your own sight, for your iniquities and your abominations.*
> *32 Not for your sake do I do this," says YHWH Elohim, "let it be known to you. Be ashamed and confounded for your own ways, O House of Israel!"*

In his flesh, man is basically lazy, and he does not do anything unless he sees a need. That being the case, why would the Ephraimite people leave the comfort and safety of America, and go to a land that will lie in ruins in the wake of a major war?

We can only guess as to why the Ephraimites will want to leave all the comforts and safety of home, but one reason might be that it may no longer be quite so comfortable, or safe. The Ephraimites originally came to America to escape persecution, and it seems likely that YHWH will re-create persecution, in order to get Ephraim to want to go home.

As the Harry Potter generation continues to come into voting age, and as Americans continue to turn away from the same Judeo-Christian traditions that originally made America great, how likely is it that those who truly believe in His Word would elect to settle in the newly annexed territories, if it meant they could live out their faith without persecution?

In the wake of a major war in which the Americans and their allies helped Israel to overcome their Islamic foes, how likely would the Israelis be to open their doors to American and allied Christian settlement, especially seeing as they will need to occupy these newly annexed lands with *someone*; and why not with the same people who just stood by them in a war?

Christian groups continue to build political alliances within Israel, to the extent that the Christians have even established a political association within the Knesset itself. Further, the Israeli public is finally becoming aware of their longstanding persecution of Christianity within their own borders. Israelis are starting to ask why they allow virtually any kind of Jew to immigrate to the Land of Israel, except believers in Yeshua.

And how likely will Judah be to accept his Messiah, when he sees that the country that just helped him win a regional war with Islam (i.e., America) is also the home of the Ephraimite people; and that the Ephraimite people have also gathered themselves together and *taken* a Stick, just as Ezekiel foretold?

> *Yehezqel (Ezekiel) 37:16b-17*
> *16b Then take another stick and write on it, 'For Joseph, the Stick of Ephraim, and for all the House of Israel, his companions.'*

17 Then join them one to another for yourself into one stick, and they will become one in your hand.

While it is true that Zionism was first founded upon the desire to escape from Christian persecution, the world of today differs considerably from the world of 1896 (or even the world of 1948). Religious and non-religious Israelis alike were startled when America's Protestant Christians threatened to turn President George W. Bush out of office, if he failed to adequately support Israel in the Palestinian conflict.

Moreover, the average Israeli is becoming aware that the reason that America has so long stood by Israel is principally because of its Christians. Although the official immigration policy in Israel is still against allowing believers in Yeshua to come into the Land in any form, this policy is beginning to come under widespread criticism in the Land. Many Israelis are starting to ask why their establishment is so steadfastly against belief in Yeshua, and yet the doors for immigration are open to Jews of any other religious persuasion (including witchcraft, Buddhism, Hinduism and even Satanism). The average man on the street in Israel is starting to wonder how his nation can justify a continued policy of discrimination against the same people who have supported their nation through more than a half a century of Muslim onslaught.

If Judah and Joseph fight together successfully, how difficult would it be for the average Israeli to allow American Christians to settle in his land? Zechariah clearly says that a 'mixed race' (which is an apt description of Ephraim) will settle in Ashdod (which lies just south of Tel Aviv, but north of the Gaza Strip).

> *Zechariah 9:6*
> *6 "A mixed race shall settle in Ashdod, And I will cut off the pride of the Philistines (the Palestinians).*

And perhaps speaking of a metaphorical (spiritual) land of Egypt and Assyria, YHWH tells us that those of Ephraim will be gathered in from far countries.

> *Zechariah 10:7-10*
> *7 Those of Ephraim shall be like a mighty man, and their heart shall rejoice as if with wine. Yes, their children shall see it and be glad; their heart shall rejoice in YHWH.*
> *8 I will whistle for them and gather them, for I will redeem them; and they shall increase as they once increased.*
> *9 "I will sow them among the peoples, and they shall remember Me in far countries. They shall live, together with their children, and they shall return.*
> *10 I will also bring them back from the land of Egypt, and gather them from Assyria. I will bring them into the land of Gilead and Lebanon, until no more room is found for them.*

What is so exciting is that these days appear to be close at hand. And, while we do not know whether it will take place before, during or after the Ingathering, Zechariah also tells us that YHWH will pour out a spirit of supplication and prayer, and cause Judah to realize that Yeshua really is the Messiah.

> **Zechariah 12:10**
> 10 "And I will pour on the House of David and on the inhabitants of Jerusalem the Spirit of grace and supplication; then they will look on Me whom they pierced. Yes, they will mourn for Him as one mourns for his only son, and grieve for Him as one grieves for a firstborn.

At whatever point it takes place, once it becomes clear to Judah that the Ephraimites are coming out from Christendom, and that the *reason* for Joseph's return to the Covenant is precisely his faith in Yeshua, the average Jew will no longer be able to escape the inevitable conclusion that Yeshua really is the Messiah: the Anointed One who regathers the lost and the scattered of Israel.

With both houses believing on Yeshua, with the War(s) of Territorial Expansion successfully won and the Two Houses restored to the Land, at some point there will also be a Religious Unification, and Nazarene Israel will be established as the official religion of the Millennial Land. We can also expect to see the joint electoral head mentioned in Hosea 2:2 (Hosea 1:11 in English versions) be inaugurated, whether he be called a president, a prime minister, or whatever other title.

> **Hosea 2:2 (1:11 in English versions)**
> 2 Then the children of Judah and the children of Israel shall be gathered together, and appoint for themselves one head; and they shall come up out of the land, for great will be the day of Jezre'el!

The faith for which Yeshua was crucified from before the foundations of the world will ultimately prevail, and the Two Houses shall come together. However, lest we forget: before Ephraim can go home, he must meet certain legal pre-requisites. Until Ephraim comes back together and forms the Stick (or Nation) of Ephraim, the Ingathering cannot take place.

There are those who are confident that since it is YHWH's Word, His Word shall be accomplished, with or without any help from us humans. And, while this is certainly the case, it is also true that YHWH has His eyes on us all. He knows who is working to help fulfill His prophetic Word, and who is sacrificing to help establish His Son's empire here on earth, and who is not; and He promises to repay each according to his works.

We will talk about what Ephraim has to do to fulfill his part of the bargain in the final chapters of this book: but before we do that, first let us clarify what happens to us after we go to stand before the throne, and our deeds (good, bad, or nonexistent) are recounted.

New Heavens, New Earth

We have already seen that Yeshua cannot return at the start of the Millennium. However, if Yeshua does not return at the start of the Millennium to give everyone an immortal body, then how do we explain verses such as Isaiah 65:20, which tells us that there will come a time when a child will die at a hundred years of age, and still be considered 'young'?

> *Yeshayahu (Isaiah) 65:20*
> *20 "No more shall an infant from there live but a few days, nor an old man who has not fulfilled his days; for the child shall die one hundred years old, But the sinner being one hundred years old shall be accursed."*

Believing that this verse applies to the Millennium, some believers start to wonder how can a child die at a hundred years old, and still be considered a 'child,' if we are still to have these same types of mortal bodies during the Millennium. How does that work? The answer, of course, is that Isaiah 65:20 does not refer to the Millennium. Isaiah 65 refers to a time that comes *after* the Millennium, when those few who survive the Day of Judgment will go on to a 'New Earth.'

> *Yeshayahu (Isaiah) 65:17-25*
> *17 "For behold, I create new heavens and a new earth; and the former shall not be remembered or come to mind. 18 But be glad and rejoice forever in*

> *what I create; for behold, I create Jerusalem as a rejoicing, and her people a joy.*
> *19 I will rejoice in Jerusalem, and joy in My people; the voice of weeping shall no longer be heard in her, nor the voice of crying.*
> **20 "No more shall an infant from there live but a few days, nor an old man who has not fulfilled his days; for the child shall die one hundred years old, But the sinner being one hundred years old shall be accursed."**

Believing that Yeshua returns at the start of the Millennium, and that Yeshua will give all of His people supernatural bodies capable of living for a thousand years, Pre-Millennial Return Theory wrongly applies this passage to the Millennium. However, if we will but look at what this passage really says, then we should be able to see that verse seventeen clearly tells us that this passage applies not to the Millennium, but to the time frame of the New Earth (which comes only after the Day of Judgment).

The thought of living for a thousand years sitting next to Yeshua is so dear that people hate to let go of it. However, since we are already several years into the Millennium (in 2007 CE), it should be clear that we are not going to live for a thousand years in the Millennium. Therefore, what we need to recognize is that the actual time sequence Scripture speaks of is this:

1. During the Millennium, the saints rule and reign in Yeshua's stead (and with His rod of iron);

2. The Great Tribulation comes at the *end* of the Millennium (more on this in the next chapter);
3. Yeshua returns in the clouds at the *end* of the Tribulation (at the *end* of the Millennium);
4. We are not caught up to be with Yeshua until He returns in the clouds (at the very last trump);
5. *Then* we go to the Judgment; and then
6. (Finally) we go to the New Earth.

While this sequence may seem unfamiliar, and while the idea of going to a 'New Earth' may seem foreign, other passages witness to it. To see this, first notice how Revelation 20 tells us that the War of Gog and Magog will come at the end of the Millennium.

> *Gilyana (Revelation) 20:7-8*
> **7 Now when the thousand years have expired, Satan will be released from his prison**
> **8 and will go out to deceive the nations which are in the four corners of the earth, Gog and Magog, to gather them together to battle, whose number is as the sand of the sea.**

Then, three verses later, Revelation 20:11 tells us that at the end of the Millennium, we will all go to stand before YHWH's throne in the Day of Judgment.

> *Gilyana (Revelation) 20:11-15*
> **11 Then I saw a great white throne and Him who sat on it, from whose face the earth and the heaven fled away. And there was found no place for them [i.e., the old heaven, and the old earth].**

> *12a And I saw the dead, small and great, standing before Elohim; and books were opened. And another book was opened, which is the Book of Life.*
> *12b And the dead were judged according to their works, by the things which were written in the books.*
> *13 The sea gave up the dead who were in it, and Death and Hades delivered up the dead who were in them. And they were judged, each one according to his works.*
> *14 Then Death and Hades were cast into the lake of fire. This is the second death.*
> *15 And anyone not found written in the Book of Life was cast into the lake of fire.*

During the Day of Judgment, the present (defiled) heaven and earth flee away, since no more place (i.e., no more need) will be found for them.

> *11 Then I saw a great white throne and Him who sat on it, from whose face the earth and the heaven fled away. And there was found no place for them (i.e., the old heaven, and the old earth).*

Then, in the Judgment, we will be judged according to our works.

> *12b And the dead were judged according to their works, by the things which were written in the books.*

> *13 The sea gave up the dead who were in it, and Death and Hades delivered up the dead who were in them. And they were judged, each one according to his works.*

Next, the New Heavens and the New Earth appear.

> **Gilyana (Revelation) 21:1**
> *1 Then I saw a new heaven and a new earth, for the first heaven and the first earth had passed away. Also there was no more sea.*

So the actual sequence of events we have seen so far is this:

1. First comes the Millennium (on this present earth, with our defiled bodies); and then
2. Second, Yeshua physically returns in the clouds at the end of the Millennium, and takes us to the Day of Judgment. Then,
3. *After* the Day of Judgment, we go to the New Earth (where an infant will die at one hundred year of age, and still be considered 'young').

Scholars disagree as to what happens when we get to the New Earth. There are different theories, and it is difficult to know what will happen with any kind of certainty, since Scripture only speaks of these things in allegory, in parable, and in prophetic shadows. It is not our purpose here to determine exactly what will happen once we get to the New Earth, but only to show that some who survive the Judgment will go on to one.

Some scholars suggest that those who lay down their lives to build Yeshua's empire here on this earth will have shown themselves worthy to go on to the New Earth. They will have 'made the cut' (whereas those who have not labored and sacrificed will not be desired, and will therefore not 'make the cut').

Other scholars suggest that from this elect group (that 'makes the cut'), YHWH will take His bride, which will then go with Yeshua to the place that is prepared for His bride. The rest of His people Israel (who survived the Judgment, but who did not 'make the cut' for the bride) will go on to the New Earth, where they will get yet another opportunity for refinement.

It is difficult for us to know just exactly what YHWH will do in the future with any certainty. He speaks of these events only in allegory, in parable, and in prophetic shadows, so we do not have enough details to foretell these things with any kind of certainty. Also, YHWH is utterly sovereign, and He can do whatever He wants. The truth, really, is that we do not need to know, but there are some patterns that prove very interesting.

The Book of Genesis is thought to be prophetic, in that it establishes patterns that seem to repeat themselves over and over again, throughout Scripture. Since these patterns recur, is it conceivable that some of these patterns may have *already* recurred? What do we mean by this?

The Book of Genesis describes a seven day Creation Week for this present earth.

> **B'reisheet (Genesis) 2:1-3**
> **1 Thus the heavens and the earth, and all the host of them, were finished.**

> *2 And on the seventh day Elohim ended His work which He had done, and He rested on the seventh day from all His work which He had done.*
> *3 Then Elohim blessed the seventh day and sanctified it, because in it He rested from all His work which Elohim had created and made.*

The Apostle Kepha (Peter) tells us not to forget that a day in prophecy can represent a thousand earth years.

> *Kepha Bet (2nd Peter) 3:8-9*
> *8 But, beloved, do not forget this one thing: That with YHWH one day is as a thousand years, and a thousand years is as one day.*

If the Creation Week was seven days long, and if each of these days represents a thousand years, then this gives a prophetic shadow picture of a seven thousand year plan for this present earth. However, beyond the seven thousand year mark lies a 'New' Earth. There are witnesses to this in Isaiah, in Revelation, and even in the Feast of Tabernacles.

It is commonly held that the Feast of Tabernacles is an eight day festival. However, technically speaking, the Feast of Tabernacles lasts for seven days, and then it is followed by a separate one day celebration on the eighth day. This eighth-day is called "Shemini Atzeret" ('The Eighth-Day Assembly,' or 'The Last Great Day'). Let us take a look at the commandment, and see how this Eighth-Day Assembly is also representative of the New (or *Renewed*) Earth.

Vayiqra (Leviticus) 23:33-36
Then YHWH spoke to Moshe, saying,
34 "Speak to the children of Israel, saying: 'The fifteenth day of this seventh month shall be the Feast of Tabernacles for seven days to YHWH.
35 On the first day there shall be a set-apart gathering. You shall do no customary work on it.
36a For seven days you shall offer an offering made by fire to YHWH.
36b On the eighth day you shall have a set-apart gathering, and you shall offer an offering made by fire to YHWH.
36c It is a solemn assembly (עצרת), and you shall do no customary work on it."

In Hebrew, the word for 'solemn assembly' is the word 'atzeret' (עצרת). This word indicates a very special kind of assembly. It indicates that one's host is not letting one go home, but is 'holding one over' for an extended period. Strong's Concordance gives the definition for the word atzeret (עצרת) as:

> *OT:6116 `atsarah (ats-aw-raw'); or `atsereth (ats-eh'-reth); from OT:6113; an assembly, especially on a festival or holiday:*

When we look up the root word at Strong's OT:6113, we find:

> *OT:6113 `atsar (aw-tsar'); a primitive root; to enclose;*

> *by analogy, <u>to hold back</u>; also to maintain, rule, assemble:*
> *KJV - be able, close up, <u>detain</u>, fast, <u>keep</u> (self close, still), prevail, recover, refrain, reign, restrain, <u>retain</u>, shut (up), slack, stay, stop, withhold (self).*

The seven days of Tabernacles are symbolic of the seven thousand years of Earth, while the Last Great Day is a prophetic foreshadow of the New Earth, in which YHWH will 'hold over' those who have been chosen to go on to the New (or Renewed) Earth. We do not know for sure whether those who will be sent on to the New Earth are those who are chosen as the bride, or whether it will be those who 'did not quite make the bride.' However, it is clear that someone in Israel will survive the Day of Judgment, and that YHWH will 'hold them over' in a New Earth.

That the Last Great Day is a prophetic foreshadow of the New Earth answers some questions, but it leaves us with still others. For example, Revelation 21:1-4 tells us that in the New Earth, there will be no more death, for the former things will have passed away.

> *Gilyana (Revelation) 21:1-4*
> *1 Now I saw a new heaven and a new earth, for the first heaven and the first earth had passed away. Also there was no more sea.*
> *2 Then I, Yochanan, saw the set-apart city, New Jerusalem, coming down out of heaven from Elohim, prepared as a bride adorned for her husband.*
> *3 And I heard a loud voice from heaven saying, "Behold, the*

> tabernacle of Elohim is with men, and He will dwell with them, and they shall be His people. Elohim Himself will be with them, and be their Elohim.
> 4 "And Elohim will wipe away every tear from their eyes; there shall be no more death, nor sorrow, nor crying. There shall be no more pain, for the former things have passed away."

This language shadows Isaiah 65:17-19 perfectly:

> *Yeshayahu (Isaiah) 65:17-19*
> *17 "For behold, I create new heavens and a new earth; and the former shall not be remembered or come to mind.*
> *18 But be glad and rejoice forever in what I create; for behold, I create Jerusalem as a rejoicing, and her people a joy.*
> *19 I will rejoice in Jerusalem, and joy in My people. The voice of weeping shall no longer be heard in her, or the voice of crying."*

And, six verses later, Isaiah 65:25 still speaks of a blissful, Edenic-like state.

> *Yeshayahu (Isaiah) 65:25*
> *25 "The wolf and the lamb shall feed together, the lion shall eat straw like the ox, and dust shall be the serpent's food. They shall not hurt nor destroy in all My Set-apart Mountain," says YHWH.*

We do not know if these passages are to be taken literally, or if they are symbolic, but they seem to suggest that those who go on to the New Earth will enjoy a life that is far superior to the one in this world.

[Alternately, Isaiah 65:25 could be speaking of the Millennium, in that the wolf is the symbol of Benjamin (which is part of the House of Judah) and the Lamb is symbolic of Yeshua (whose cause is more-or-less championed by the House of Ephraim). The lion may symbolize Yeshua (who is part of the Tribe of Judah), while the ox may symbolize the House of Joseph (Ephraim), whose symbol was the ox. If so, then Isaiah 65:25 is actually a prophecy about peace between the Two Houses, which could pertain to the Millennium (and not the New Earth). However, this would not alter the fact that there will be a New Earth.]

These insights still leave us with some questions. While Revelation 21:4 (above) tells us that there will be no more death, Isaiah 65:20 seems to contradict this. Isaiah 65:20 tells us that there will still be death (and also sin) in the New Earth.

> **Yeshayahu (Isaiah) 65:20**
> **20 "No more shall an infant from there live but a few days, nor an old man who has not fulfilled his days; For the child shall die one hundred years old, but the sinner being one hundred years old shall be accursed."**

Not only does Isaiah 65:20 tell us that there will be sin and death in the New Earth, but Revelation Twenty-two *also* tells us that there will be sin in the New Earth (and that there will further be idolaters, and liars).

> *Gilyana (Revelation) 22:14-15*
> *14 Blessed are those who do His commandments, that they may have the right to the tree of life, and may enter through the gates into the city.*
> *15 But outside are dogs and sorcerers and sexually immoral and murderers and idolaters, and whoever loves and practices a lie.*

So how can we reconcile these passages, some of which speak of an Edenic-like state, and others of sin and death? With the few prophetic pictures we are given, it is difficult to say with certainty. However, Revelation Twenty-one does tell us that those who are selected to be 'held over' in the New Earth do not go to the New Jerusalem right away, but that the New Jerusalem comes down to earth only somewhat *later*.

> *Gilyana (Revelation) 21:1-2*
> *1 Now I saw a new heaven and a new earth, for the first heaven and the first earth had passed away. Also there was no more sea.*
> *2 Then I, Yochanan, saw the set-apart city, New Jerusalem, coming down out of heaven from Elohim, prepared as a bride adorned for her husband.*

Is it possible that once YHWH causes the Renewed Jerusalem to come down from above, that there will be created an Edenic-like state within Jerusalem itself; but that whosoever sins will be put outside of Jerusalem, where sickness and death still exist? We do not know, but this solution harmonizes with some other passages.

> *Gilyana (Revelation) 21:22-27*
> **22** *But I saw no Temple in it, for YHWH Elohim El Shaddai and the Lamb are its Temple.*
> **23** *The city had no need of the sun or of the moon to shine in it, for the glory of Elohim illuminated it. The Lamb is its light.*
> **24** *And the nations of those who are saved shall walk in its light, and the kings of the earth bring their glory and honor into it.*
> **25** *Its gates shall not be shut at all by day (there shall be no night there).*
> **26** *And they shall bring the glory and the honor of the nations into it.*
> **27** *But there shall by no means enter it anything that defiles, or causes an abomination or a lie, but only those who are written in the Lamb's Book of Life.*

Blessed are those who do all of His commandments, that they may take hold of the Tree of Life, and enter into the city (and its Edenic-like state); while outside are all those who do not keep the Torah completely.

> *Gilyana (Revelation) 22:14-15*
> **14** *Blessed are those who do His Commandments, that they may have the right to the tree of life, and may enter through the gates into the city.*
> **15** *But outside are dogs and sorcerers and sexually immoral and murderers and idolaters, and whoever loves and practices a lie.*

Since the Book of the Revelation speaks in symbolic language, we cannot know just exactly what the New Earth will be like. However, we do know that to make it into the Renewed Jerusalem means life, and *not* to make it there means death. Bearing in mind that this is an issue of eternal life or death, why would anyone *not* choose to do all he can, to build Yeshua's empire? And why would anyone *not* choose to do all he can to help Nazarene Israel build the Stick of Ephraim? With life or death at stake, is there any truly good reason?

Additionally, some scholars suggest that this present earth may itself be a kind of 'renewed' earth. What else can we say about this?

> **B'reisheet (Genesis) 1:1-2**
> **1 In the beginning Elohim created the heavens and the earth.**
> **2 The earth was made formless and void; and darkness was on the face of the deep.**

Now here is a difficult concept. In Hebrew, the word 'created' is the word 'ba-ra' (בָּרָא). This word בָּרָא means, essentially, "created from nothing." So what Genesis 1:1 tells us, then, is that Elohim created the heavens and the earth literally 'from nothing.'

In contrast, when we read that the earth 'was made' formless and void, the word is 'hay-yi-tah' (הָיְתָה). This word הָיְתָה means 'made from something else.' Some scholars therefore suggest the possibility of a lag time in between the time when YHWH 'created' (בָּרָא) the earth from nothing, and the time when the earth 'was made' (הָיְתָה) formless and void. Is there any truth to this? And if so, then what would it mean?

Let us take a look at the Hebrew of how the earth 'was made' (or 'was rendered') formless and void:

Genesis 1:2a 2a The earth was made formless and void; and darkness was on the face of the deep.	(2) וְהָאָרֶץ הָיְתָה תֹהוּ וָבֹהוּ וְחֹשֶׁךְ עַל פְּנֵי תְהוֹם

The word 'made' can also be translated as 'rendered.'

Genesis 1:2a 2a The earth was *rendered* formless and void; and darkness was on the face of the deep.	(2) וְהָאָרֶץ הָיְתָה תֹהוּ וָבֹהוּ וְחֹשֶׁךְ עַל פְּנֵי תְהוֹם

The Hebrew for "formless and void" is "tohu v'bohu" (תֹהוּ וָבֹהוּ). This phrase has been colloquially rendered as, 'tossed green salad.' It speaks to a process of complete upheaval, and being made totally desolate (or gutted), so that a renewal and refreshing can occur. The Hebrew word "tohu" (תֹהוּ) is defined as:

> **OT:8414 tohuw (תֹהוּ);** *from an unused root meaning <u>to lie waste</u>; a <u>desolation</u> (of surface), i.e. desert; figuratively, a worthless thing; adverbially, in vain: KJV - confusion, empty place, without form, nothing, (thing of) nought, vain, vanity, waste, wilderness.*

Similarly, the Hebrew word "bohu" (בֹהוּ) means:

OT:922 bohuw (בֹהוּ); *from an unused root (meaning to be empty); a vacuity, i.e. (superficially) <u>an undistinguishable ruin</u>:*
KJV - *emptiness, void.*

Next, remembering that in Hebrew, the word 'new' is actually the word 'renewed' (חָדָשׁ or חֲדָשָׁה), we can see that Isaiah 65:17 is speaking to the same concept of destruction-and-renewal that Genesis 1:2 speaks of.

| Isaiah 65:17
"For behold, I create (a) <u>renewed</u> heavens and a <u>renewed</u> earth;
And the former shall not be remembered or come to mind." | (17) כִּי הִנְנִי בוֹרֵא שָׁמַיִם חֲדָשִׁים וָאָרֶץ חֲדָשָׁה ׀ וְלֹא תִזָּכַרְנָה הָרִאשֹׁנוֹת וְלֹא תַעֲלֶינָה עַל לֵב |

Bearing all of these things in mind, some theologians have suggested that the earth may have already been 'renewed' back when the earth was first rendered (or made) "tohu v'bohu" (back in Genesis 1:2).

| Genesis 1:2a
2a The earth was *rendered* formless and void; and darkness was on the face of the deep. | (2) וְהָאָרֶץ הָיְתָה תֹהוּ וָבֹהוּ וְחֹשֶׁךְ עַל פְּנֵי תְהוֹם |

We do not know if the earth was 'renewed' at the start of this present seven thousand year period, but if so, then there might be some interesting parallels between the Scriptural record of creation and renewal, and the philosophies of creation-and-renewal found in some eastern religions. This would not be to condone or support these eastern religions in any way (as they are heretical). However, it might explain a few things.

In the Book of Genesis, when Avraham wanted to give his inheritance to Yitzhak (Isaac), he sent his other sons away eastward, to the "land of the east."

> **B'reisheet (Genesis) 25:5-6**
> **5 And Avraham gave all that he had to Yitzhak.**
> **6 But Avraham gave gifts to the sons of the concubines which Avraham had; and while he was still living he sent them eastward, away from Isaac his son, to the land of the east.**

Technically, this "land of the east" is Haran, but it does indicate an eastward pattern of migration that is similar to the northward pattern of migrations that the House of Ephraim later followed. It indicates a direction.

In Scriptural thought, everything has origins, and a beginning. If Avraham understood that there would be a New Earth, and then he sent his sons away eastward (to the "land of the east"), then could this explain why the Hindu religious caste is known as the *Brahmins*? Could it be that these Brahmins are really the *Abramins* (i.e., the descendants of Abram/Abraham)? If so, might this explain why Hinduism also teaches a religious tradition that speaks of creation and renewal?

In Hebraic thought, everything has origins, and a beginning. Can we therefore also trace the possible beginnings of Chinese Taoism?

In a book called the "Tao Te Ching," the Taoist sages are recorded as 'just appearing' one day, as from afar, being endowed with unusually great spiritual wisdom. Is it possible that these could have been some of the other sons that Avraham sent away eastward, to the "land(s) of the east"?

The Chinese word for Zen spiritual enlightenment is Chan (or Chen), which is similar to the Hebrew word for Favor, or Grace (which is Chen, or חן). We could also note that in Chinese, the word for life force (or life energy) is Chi, which is similar to the Hebrew word for life, which is Chai (or חי). Is it possible that these words are corrupt derivatives of the Aramaic terms that Avraham taught to his sons?

If Chinese Taoism and Hindu really are corrupt variants of the Avrahamic faith, then this would not lend any credence to Taoism or Hindu. However, it might explain some of the many parallels that exist between the Israelite faith, and Taoism, Hindu and Buddhism (which arose from Hindu).

Both in Buddhism and in Hinduism, a person is thought to be sent into the material realm because of his 'attachments' (or desires) for certain pleasures in the material realm. Examples of desires that need to be overcome can be greed for material objects, sexual desires, control issues, or what-have-you). We should be able to see that this is more-or-less parallel to what the Apostle Yochanan (John) tells, which is that all that is in the world is the lust of the eyes, the lust of the flesh, and the pride of life (First John 2:16-17).

Hinduism and Buddhism also teach that when one finally overcomes one's desires, one no longer returns to this world. Since one has become purified, one can now progress onward to other worlds which are purer, and more satisfying. If this doctrine really is a corrupt variation of the original Avrahamic faith, and if the original Avrahamic faith understood that there would one day be a New Earth, then could this explain why the Book of the Revelation also teaches that life in the New Earth will be more satisfying than this one?

> *Gilyana (Revelation) 22:1-5*
> *1 And he showed me a pure river of water of life, clear as crystal, proceeding from the throne of Elohim, and of the Lamb.*
> *2 In the middle of its street, and on either side of the river, was the tree of life, which bore twelve fruits, each tree yielding its fruit every month. The leaves of the tree were for the healing of the nations.*
> *3 And there shall be no more curse, but the throne of Elohim and of the Lamb shall be in it, and His servants shall serve Him.*
> *4 They shall see His face, and His name shall be on their foreheads.*
> *5 There shall be no night there: They need no lamp nor light of the sun, for YHWH Elohim gives them light.*
> *And they shall reign forever and ever.*

Many may misunderstand what we are saying here, so in order to avoid confusion, let us say a word more about these things.

The reason for pointing these things out is not that we want to lend any credence to Hinduism, Buddhism or Taoism: far from it. The author was delivered from these faiths, and so he knows first hand how empty and devoid of Salvation they truly are. However, it may be helpful for some people to know why parallels exist between what Scripture teaches, and the beliefs of these eastern faiths.

Many of the Ephraimite people are being lost to these eastern faiths, and to the New Age cultic religions. Some of these get lost because they are impressed at the parallels between Scripture and the religions of the east. This is because they do not realize that the religions of the east are merely corrupt variations of the faith that Avraham originally taught to his other sons.

Further, many ex-Christians believe that the Nazarene faith is just for Christians: Elohim forbid. There are many in China and India who are turning to Scripture, and the Sabbath movement is gaining strength there. Are their lives any less precious in Elohim's eyes, than our own? Can we afford not to draft materials that witness to those in the east, who are being saved?

Could it be that by understanding why there are so many parallels between Scripture and the religious systems of the east, that we may be able to reach out to those who are presently lost in these faiths, so that Yeshua's prophecy about *many* coming both from east and from west might be more completely fulfilled?

> ***Mattai (Matthew) 8:11***
> ***11 And I say to you that many will come from east and west, and sit down with Avraham, Yitzhak, and Ya'akov in the kingdom of heaven.***

Finally, some suggest that we should not even mention these parallels, because Scripture commands us not to mention the names of other elohim.

> **Shemote (Exodus) 23:13**
> **13 And in all things that I have said unto you, take heed, and make no mention of the name of other elohim, neither let it be heard out of your mouth.**

It is true that we must not mention the names of false elohim unless we have a reason. However, let us recognize that even YHWH uses the names of other elohim in Scripture, when He has a purpose for doing so.

> **Vayiqra (Leviticus) 18:21**
> **21 And you shall not give any of your seed to make them pass through the fire to Molech; neither shall you profane the name of your Elohim: I am YHWH.**

Further, we know that Yeshua is Elohim, and even Yeshua mentions Satan's name, when He has a purpose in doing so.

> **Gilyana (Revelation) 2:13**
> **13 I know where you dwell, even where Satan's throne is; and you hold fast My name, and did not deny My faith, even in the days of Antipas My witness, My faithful one, who was killed among you, where Satan dwells.**

Zechariah 12-14 Explained

Scripture tells us that certain books have been 'sealed up' until specific points in time.

> **Daniel 12:9**
> **9 And he said, "Go your way, Daniel, for the words are closed up and sealed till the time of the end."**

But how does YHWH 'seal up' certain books until set points in time? What chain of events does YHWH put in motion, that we cannot 'open' these books? In this chapter, we will discover the answer to this question.

> **Mishle (Proverbs) 25:2**
> **2 It is the glory of Elohim to conceal a matter; but the glory of kings is to search out a matter.**

Proverbs 25:2 tells us that Elohim derives glory from concealing matters (for a time, and for a purpose). So from whom does Elohim conceal these matters? It can only be from His people Israel.

But why would a kind and loving Elohim conceal matters from His people? Well, one reason might be that YHWH knows it is ultimately good for us to labor and struggle for knowledge, since these struggles increase our strength. Moreover, studying causes our overall levels of knowledge to increase.

> **Daniel 12:4**

> *4 "But you, Daniel, shut up the words, and seal the book until the time of the end; many shall run to and fro, and knowledge shall increase."*

Proverbs 25:2 tells us, then, that kings can establish glory for themselves by searching out the matters of Elohim. Let's look at it again.

> *Mishle (Proverbs) 25:2*
> *2 It is the glory of Elohim to conceal a matter; but the glory of kings is to search out a matter.*

But who are these kings who are being glorified?

Israel is supposed to be a nation of kings and priests.

> *Kepha Aleph (1st Peter) 2:9*
> *9 But you are a chosen generation, a royal priesthood, a set-apart nation, His own special people, that you may proclaim the praises of Him who called you out of darkness into His marvelous light....*

When we seek out the matters of Elohim, we are not taking YHWH's glory away from Him (as if such a thing were even possible). Rather, what happens is that YHWH has set aside a special kind of 'human' glory, specially designed for those few human beings who successfully search out the secret matters of His Word, and teach them to His people.

Why is this of importance to us? Is it because we want glory? Elohim forbid! Our motivation in searching out His Word must only be to teach the hidden things of Scripture to His people. It can be nothing else!

If any man desires to seek out the secrets of Scripture so as to glorify himself, YHWH will hide the true secrets of Scripture from him, and give him false revelations, instead. But how can this happen?

As we explored in *Nazarene Israel*, if one reads the Renewed Covenant superficially (as most Christians do), one can easily take the wrong impression. If one reads with the wrong *spirit*, one can easily believe that the Messiah came to do away with the Torah.

Many passages in the Renewed Covenant clearly tell us that the Messiah did not come to do away with the Torah, but since the standard Christian practice has become to 'skim' any passage that they do not readily understand, the Renewed Covenant has been 'sealed up' to the average Christian reader.

The same kind of phenomenon applies to end-time studies. If one fails to study carefully, one can easily take the mistaken impression that Yeshua returns to earth in physical form at the start of the Millennium. However, upon studying matters more closely, we are shown that Pre-Millennial Return Theory just leaves too many verses unexplained.

The Church (including the Messianic organizations) has read Zechariah too fast. As a result of this, the Church has taught a great many people that Zechariah Twelve through Fourteen gives us 'proof' of a Pre-Millennial Return. All of this has come because Zechariah has been 'sealed up' to their wrong spirit.

Before we begin our discussion, let us remember that originally, there was no numbering system in Scripture. Rather, YHWH inspired His prophets to speak, and the prophets wrote down all of the words that YHWH gave them in one long string (on a scroll, or in a book). They also wrote without numbering, or punctuation.

In order to make it easier to read and study Scripture, commentators in the Middle Ages divided up Scripture up into chapter-and-verse. Then they placed chapter divisions in the places where they thought best. While these commentators did a fairly good job overall, there are many places where their lack of understanding of end time events caused them to number the passages in such a way as to cause a great many readers to stumble at pre-millennialism later on. As we shall see, this is very much the case in Zechariah.

In order to understand why the commentators got confused, let us recognize that YHWH does not give prophecy in chronological order. Prophecy does not say, "First this will happen, and then that will happen." Rather, while prophecy is typically sequential *within* passages, the sequence *between* these passages is usually all scrambled up. Therefore, the commentators could not always tell which prophecies belonged to which chronological time periods.

Prophecy is all jumbled up, as if YHWH gave His people one vast jigsaw puzzle all in a heap. He did not bother to identify which passage belonged to what time period, but allowed His nation of kings and priests to earn glory for themselves by figuring out what parts of the puzzle go where. And, just like children arguing about a puzzle in the material realm, commentators and scholars have debated as to which piece of the puzzle goes where for ages.

The problem in figuring the jigsaw puzzle out is the same in Renewed (New) Covenant as it is in the prophecies. Just as it is easier to take Torahless Christianity from the Renewed Covenant, it is also easier to get Pre-Millennial Return Theory from the prophecies. And, just as Torahless Christianity asks us to throw away about a third of the pieces of the puzzle, Pre-Millennial Return Theory also asks us to ignore about fully one-third of the Text.

By giving Scripture to Israel as one big jumbled mass, YHWH sealed up the secrets of Scripture, for a time. It was not possible to know what Zechariah meant until the Two House Theory was understood; and in turn, the Two House Theory could not be understood until the prophecies over the Two Houses had been fulfilled. However, now that we understand the Two Houses of Israel, we can *also* begin to unscramble the puzzle that is Zechariah Twelve through Fourteen.

As we shall soon see, one has to be extremely careful when interpreting Zechariah, in that YHWH intentionally causes the text to jump from the Millennium's start, to the Millennium's end, to the first century, and back and forth (however He pleases).

YHWH hides the definitions of certain words, and He even changes the meanings of the same word from verse to verse within the same chronological passage. This is one means by which YHWH has brilliantly kept Zechariah 'sealed up' until now.

In "The Millennial Land" (above), we showed how Zechariah Nine through Ten prophesy victory over the Muslim people at the Millennium's start. Two chapters later, Zechariah Chapter Twelve is still speaking of events that take place at the start of the Millennium.

Zechariah Chapters 12-14
12:1 The burden of the word of YHWH against Israel:
Thus says YHWH, who stretches out the heavens, lays the foundation of the earth, and forms the spirit of man within him:
2 "Behold, I will make Jerusalem a cup of drunkenness to all the surrounding peoples, when they lay siege against Judah and Jerusalem."

Proponents of a pre-millennial return attempt to use verse 2 to justify their belief that the United Nations will attack Israel at the start of the Millennium. However, notice that verse 2 does not say that the United Nations will attack Israel at the start of the Millennium. Rather it says that the *surrounding peoples* (the Muslim nations) will be the ones to attack it.

YHWH then allows the pre-millennial return theorists to mistranslate the Hebrew of verse 3, in order to support their misinterpretation of verse 2.

| 3 And it shall happen in that day that I will make Jerusalem a very heavy stone for all peoples; all who would heave it away will surely be cut in pieces, though all nations of the *Land* are gathered against it. | (3) וְהָיָה בַיּוֹם הַהוּא אָשִׂים אֶת יְרוּשָׁלַם אֶבֶן מַעֲמָסָה לְכָל הָעַמִּים כָּל עֹמְסֶיהָ שָׂרוֹט יִשָּׂרֵטוּ ׀ וְנֶאֶסְפוּ עָלֶיהָ כֹּל גּוֹיֵי הָאָרֶץ |

Most English translations were written by Protestant Christians, who typically hold a pre-millennialist bias. Coming from their pre-millennial bias, these Protestant translators try to tell us that all the nations of the *world* will be gathered against Israel. For example:

> **Zechariah 12:3**
> **3 "It will come about in that day that I will make Jerusalem a heavy stone for all the peoples; all who lift it will be severely injured. And all the nations of the earth (הָאָרֶץ) will be gathered against it."** NASU

The problem with the NASU is the same as with most other English versions. The word 'earth' is actually "HaAretz" (הָאָרֶץ), meaning "the *Land* (of Israel)."

Verse 3 really does not say that all nations of the earth will attack Israel, but that all of the nations of the *Land* (meaning those peoples presently occupying the future Millennial Land [i.e., the Muslim nations]) will attack Israel. Therefore, what verse 3 really says is that when the Muslim nations attempt to heave Jerusalem away, these Muslim nations (and not the United Nations) will be cut in pieces. This is logical and sensible, and does not require us to believe anything that cannot be readily supported by a good close look at the daily news. It requires no stretch of the imagination.

> **4 "In that day," says YHWH,"I will strike every horse with confusion, and its rider with madness; I will open My eyes on the House of Judah, and will strike every horse of the (surrounding) peoples with blindness."**

YHWH is telling us the same thing we learned in the chapter, "The Millennial Land:" in this war, YHWH is going to bless the House of Judah, but strike the eyes of the Muslim armies with blindness.

> **5 "And the governors of Judah shall say in their heart, 'The inhabitants of Jerusalem are my strength in YHWH of hosts, their Elohim.'"**

One might at first think that the "inhabitants of Jerusalem" here might be the religious Orthodox Jews. However, as we will see in verse 6 (below), this cannot be the case. Rather, it can only be a reference to a group of *people* (i.e., a 'spiritual' Jerusalem) because we are told that Jerusalem will once again inhabit her own *place* (i.e., physical Jerusalem).

> **6 "In that day I will make the governors of Judah like a fire-pan in the woodpile, and like a fiery torch in the sheaves; they shall devour all the surrounding peoples on the right hand and on the left, but Jerusalem shall be inhabited again in her own place — (physical) Jerusalem."**

Who are these people called (spiritual) Jerusalem, who will inhabit the physical Jerusalem? It cannot be the religious Orthodox, because they already inhabit the city of Jerusalem. Therefore, it must be *some other* group of people: but who? The answer is probably the American (and possibly also the British) Christians, for reasons we will see below. (And, as we will see, the Nazarenes may be the spiritual House of David.)

Given the political turn of events in recent years, it may be that when the Muslim nations attack Israel, Israel's elected officials will see that the main reason America supports Israel is because of America's Protestant Christians. Therefore, these astonished governors of Israel will say to themselves, "The American Christians are our strength in YHWH of hosts...who is also *their* Elohim!"

> **5 "And the governors of Judah shall say in their heart, 'The inhabitants of Jerusalem are my strength in YHWH of hosts, (who is also) their Elohim!'"**

Next we see a reference to a spiritual *House of David*, as well as another reference to 'spiritual' Jerusalem.

> **7 "YHWH will save the tents of Judah first, so that the glory of the House of David and the glory of the inhabitants of (spiritual) Jerusalem shall not become greater than that of Judah."**

The *House of David* and the *inhabitants of Jerusalem* here cannot be Jewish, because YHWH says He will save the tents of Judah first (so that Judah's glory will not be outdone by that of the American [and perhaps the British] Christians).

> **8 "In that day YHWH will defend the inhabitants of Jerusalem; the one who is feeble among them in that day shall be like David, and the House of David shall be like Elohim, like the malach (messenger) of YHWH before them."**

159

In order to 'seal up' this passage, YHWH intentionally had Zechariah speak of the inhabitants of the *physical* Jerusalem here. By switching between physical and spiritual, YHWH made it so the true meaning of this passage could not be understood until the modern day.

> **9 "It shall be in that day that I will seek to destroy all the nations that come against Jerusalem."**

Alternately, verse 9 might be a reference *both* to physical *and* spiritual Jerusalem (i.e., Israel and the pro-Israeli Christians). YHWH might be saying that He will seek to destroy anyone who comes against *either* of His Two Houses, Israel and/or Judah.

However, in the next verse, the terms *House of David* and *inhabitants of Jerusalem* are references to Judah. YHWH intentionally switches the definitions back and forth here, in order to 'seal up' Zechariah until such time as the Two Houses were understood, and the Stick of Ephraim was ready to be built.

> **10 "And I will pour on the House of David and on the inhabitants of Jerusalem the Spirit of grace and supplication; then they will look on Me whom they pierced. Yes, they will mourn for Him as one mourns for his only son, and grieve for Him as one grieves for a firstborn."**

Imagine the depth of Judah's remorse when he realizes they he was the one used to put Yeshua to death (so that no man might boast of his heritage).

> *11 "In that day there shall be a great mourning in Jerusalem, like the mourning at Hadad Rimon in the plain of Megiddo.*
> *12 And the Land shall mourn, every family by itself: the family of the House of David by itself, and their wives by themselves; the family of the house of Nathan by itself, and their wives by themselves;*
> *13 the family of the House of Levi by itself, and their wives by themselves; the family of Shimei by itself, and their wives by themselves;*
> *14 all the families that remain, every family by itself, and their wives by themselves."*

Given the fact that YHWH does not waste words, that YHWH would spend four whole verses describing the depth of Judah's mourning tells us that it will be a very great mourning indeed.

When exactly this great mourning will take place, we do not know. However, we can surmise from other verses in Scripture that it will come about as a result of the reformation of the Stick of Ephraim. When this great event finally does take place, it should pave the way for the Ingathering of the Exiles, as well as the settlement of the lands newly freed from Muslim occupation (in the War [or Wars] of Territorial Expansion).

> *13:1 "In that day a fountain shall be opened for the House of David and for the inhabitants of Jerusalem, for sin and for uncleanness."*

The Ruach Qodesh (the Set-apart Spirit) is described as water, and we can guess that this 'fountain' will be an outpouring of the Set-apart Spirit (also alluded to in Zechariah 12:10, above).

> **2 "It shall be in that day," says YHWH of hosts, "that I will cut off the names of the idols from the land, and they shall no longer be remembered. I will also cause the prophets and the unclean spirit to depart from the land."**

In *Nazarene Israel*, we discussed the idols of the House of Ephraim; namely, the crosses, the steeples, the images of doves, the images of Yeshua, the so-called 'menorah fish,' and so forth. However, Ephraim is not alone in using false religious images. The House of Judah *also* uses numerous religious images, such as the Star of David (i.e., the Star of Remphan/Star of Kiyyun), and others. Moreover, Judah tends to exalt (and even worship) men, valuing the traditions and teachings of men (in the Talmud) more than the Torah of YHWH (see also Matthew 15:1-9). These will depart from the Land. Moreover, the next verse tells us that after Judah becomes saved, the rabbis will no longer 'prophesy' falsehood (and indeed, people will probably no longer even call themselves 'rabbi.')

> **3 "It shall come to pass that if anyone still prophesies, then his father and mother who begot him will say to him, 'You shall not live, because you have spoken lies in the name of YHWH.' And his father and mother who begot him shall thrust him through when he prophesies.**

> *4 And it shall be in that day that every prophet will be ashamed of his vision when he prophesies; they will not wear a robe of coarse hair to deceive.*
> *5 But he will say, 'I am no prophet, I am a farmer; for a man taught me to keep cattle from my youth.'*
> *6 And one will say to him, 'What are these wounds between your arms?' Then he will answer, 'Those with which I was wounded in the house of my friends.'"*

One wonders why the commentators put the chapter division where they did (above, at verse 1), because the place it really belongs is here, at the end of verse 6. The reason the chapter division belongs here is that we now shift to the *first* century time frame.

> *Zechariah 13:7*
> *7 "Awake, O sword, against My Shepherd, against the Man who is My Companion," says YHWH of hosts. "Strike the Shepherd, and the sheep will be scattered: Then I will turn My hand against the little ones."*

Scripture tells us plainly that this verse was fulfilled in Yeshua's time. (See also Mark 14:27-31, Luke 22:31-34, and John 13:36-38.)

> *Mattai (Matthew) 26:31*
> *31 Then Yeshua said to them, "All of you will be made to stumble because of Me this night, for it is written:*

> *'I will strike the Shepherd, and the sheep of the flock will be scattered.'"*

Next, we need to understand that while the phrase, "In that day" indicates that a specific event will take place at a certain *time*, the phrase, "and it shall come to pass" indicates that an event will come to pass *over many years*. Not realizing this, pre-millennial return theorists teach that verses eight and nine refer to *today's* time, because they believe that the United Nations will attack Israel very soon. The problem with their interpretation is that this passage was fulfilled by the Romans at the time of the destruction of the Temple (in 70 CE), and during Judah's crushing defeat at the time of the Bar Kochba Revolt. These are ancient (and not pre-millennial) events.

> *8 And it shall come to pass in all the land," says YHWH, "that two-thirds in it shall be cut off and die, but one-third shall be left in it:*
> *9 I will bring the one-third through the fire, will refine them as silver is refined, and test them as gold is tested. They will call on My Name, and I will answer them. I will say, 'This is My people,' and each one will say, 'YHWH is my Elohim.'"*

Verses 8 and 9 tell us that those Jews who were left at the end of the Roman devastation (and the subsequent Exile) would be brought into severe refinement, and that two-thirds of Judah would be cut off from the Land (and die) over the course of several centuries. It would not be a singular event, but it would 'come to pass.'

Next, Zechariah Chapter Fourteen marks a departure from the ancient time frame, and jumps to the end of the Millennium. However, before we look at Zechariah, let us review what we learned in Revelation.

As we already saw (in the chapters above), Revelation 20:7-9 tells us that the War of Gog and Magog will take place at the *end* of the Millennium.

> *Gilyana (Revelation) 20:7-9*
> *7 Now when the thousand years have expired, Satan will be released from his prison*
> *8 and will go out to deceive the nations which are in the four corners of the earth, Gog and Magog, to gather them together to battle, whose number is as the sand of the sea.*
> *9 They went up on the breadth of the earth and surrounded the camp of the saints and the beloved city. And fire came down from Elohim out of heaven and devoured them.*

Notice, then, how perfectly Revelation 20 meshes with Yeshua's triumphal return in Zechariah Fourteen, which tells us that when Jerusalem is besieged by all the nations of the world (Gog and Magog), that YHWH Himself (i.e., Yeshua) will come to the rescue:

| Zechariah 14:1-2
1 Behold, the day of YHWH is coming, And your spoil will be divided in your midst. | (1) הִנֵּה יוֹם בָּא
לַיהוָה ׀ וְחֻלַּק שְׁלָלֵךְ
בְּקִרְבֵּךְ : |

| 2 For I will gather all the nations to battle against Jerusalem. The city shall be taken, the houses rifled, and the women ravished. Half of the city shall go into captivity, but the remnant of the people shall not be cut off from the city (meaning they will probably be enslaved.) | (2) וְאָסַפְתִּי אֶת כָּל הַגּוֹיִם אֶל יְרוּשָׁלַם לַמִּלְחָמָה וְנִלְכְּדָה הָעִיר וְנָשַׁסּוּ הַבָּתִּים וְהַנָּשִׁים תשגלנה [תִּשָּׁכַבְנָה קרי] וְיָצָא חֲצִי הָעִיר בַּגּוֹלָה וְיֶתֶר הָעָם לֹא יִכָּרֵת מִן הָעִיר |

In contrast to how Zechariah Chapter Twelve tells us that the surrounding nations (i.e., the Muslim nations) will attack Israel, the language in Zechariah Fourteen tells us that Satan really will marshal all the nations of the world against Israel, just as Revelation also says.

The language here reads כָּל הַגּוֹיִם, "all the nations." However, this battle against all the nations of the world takes place at the *end* of the Millennium (as Revelation also says).

In context, then, after Israel has ruled and reigned with Yeshua in their hearts for a thousand years, Satan will be released from the Pit (with a vengeance). When this happens, Satan will amass armies so strong that Israel will not be able to stand (but will be overrun).

When Israel is finally overrun in the Great Tribulation, the city will be ransacked, and the women sexually assaulted. The situation will be so desperate that the only thing that will save poor Israel is the triumphal return of her Husband, the Conquering King.

> *Zechariah 14:3-4*
> *3 Then YHWH (Yeshua) will go forth and fight against those nations, as He fights in the day of battle.*
> *4 And in that day His feet will stand on the Mount of Olives, which faces Jerusalem on the east; and the Mount of Olives shall be split in two, from east to west, making a very large valley. Half of the mountain shall move toward the north, and half of it toward the south.*

Verse 5 tells us that some in Israel will not be caught up to be with Yeshua at His coming, but that they will have to undertake flight through the mountain valley. This shows us that not all of Israel will be taken as part of His bride (see also the Parable of the Ten Virgins at Matthew 25:1-13).

> *Zechariah 14:5*
> *5 Then you shall flee through My mountain valley, for the mountain valley shall reach to Azal. Yes, you shall flee as you fled from the earthquake in the days of Uzziah king of Judah. Thus YHWH my Elohim (i.e., Yeshua in the clouds) will come; and all the saints with You.*

When the Conquering King returns in the clouds, He will call down fire from heaven upon Satan's armies.

> *Gilyana (Revelation) 20:9b*
> *9b And fire came down from Elohim out of heaven and devoured them.*

Notice the parallel to how Yeshua called down fire and brimstone upon Satan's armies in the destruction of Sodom and Gomorrah.

> **B'reisheet (Genesis) 19:24**
> **24 Then YHWH rained brimstone and fire on Sodom and Gomorrah, from YHWH out of the heavens.**

After Yeshua has caught His bride up to be with Him and He has smitten the enemies of Israel, the very next thing that happens is that we will all go to stand before the great white throne in the Day of Judgment, where our reward will be determined according to our works.

> **Gilyana (Revelation) 20:11-12**
> **11 Then I saw a great white throne and Him who sat on it, from whose face the earth and the heaven fled away. And there was found no place for them.**
> **12 And I saw the dead, small and great, standing before Elohim, and books were opened. And another book was opened, which is the Book of Life. And the dead were judged according to their works, by the things which were written in the books.**

Many people find it difficult to imagine how they can stop living their lives in the world, and make service to YHWH their number one priority in life. How can they find time to build the Stick of Ephraim? These would do well to remember that the only thing that will matter when we stand before His throne is how much we did to help build His Son's empire, here on earth.

After the Judgment, 'it shall come to pass' (over many generations) that those who are found worthy will go forward to the Renewed Earth, where there will be no light; and that it will be neither day nor night.

> **Zechariah 14:6-7**
> **6 It shall come to pass in that day that there will be no light; the lights will diminish.**
> **7 It shall be one day which is known to YHWH — neither day nor night; but at evening time it shall happen that it will be light.**

Notice the perfect parallels to Revelation Chapter 21, which tells us how the Renewed Jerusalem (in the Renewed Earth) will have no need of a sun or moon, and how there will be no night there (since we will be spiritual beings, rather than material ones):

> **Gilyana (Revelation) 21:22-26**
> **22 But I saw no temple in it, for YHWH Elohim El Shaddai and the Lamb are its temple.**
> **23 The city had no need of the sun or of the moon to shine in it, for the glory of Elohim illuminated it. The Lamb is its light.**
> **24 And the nations of those who are saved shall walk in its light, and the kings of the earth bring their glory and honor into it.**
> **25 Its gates shall not be shut at all by day (there shall be no night there).**
> **26 And they shall bring the glory and the honor of the nations into it.**

Next, to keep the book of Zechariah sealed up, YHWH shifts gears back to the Millennium's *start*.

The reference to 'living waters' is symbolic of Yeshua and the 'living waters' of His Spirit, which will truly begin to go forth (i.e., freely flow) from Mount Zion after the Two Houses are reunited.

> ***Zechariah 14:8-21***
> ***8 And in that day it shall be that living waters shall flow from Jerusalem, half of them toward the eastern sea and half of them toward the western sea. In both summer and winter it shall occur.***
> ***9 And YHWH shall be King over all the earth. In that day it shall be — "YHWH is one," and His Name one.***
> ***10 All the land shall be turned into a plain from Geba to Rimon south of Jerusalem. Jerusalem shall be raised up and inhabited in her place from Benjamin's Gate to the place of the First Gate and the Corner Gate, and from the Tower of Hananel to the king's winepresses.***
> ***11 The people shall dwell in it; and no longer shall there be utter destruction, But Jerusalem shall be safely inhabited.***

Next, verse 12 shifts back to the war with Islam, speaking of the 'plague' that strikes the (Islamic) forces which will attack Israel. Many scholars have noted the similarity to the effects of tactical nuclear ('neutron') munitions (which America sold Israel many years ago).

> *12 And this shall be the plague with which YHWH will strike all the (Islamic) people who fought against Jerusalem: Their flesh shall dissolve while they stand on their feet, their eyes shall dissolve in their sockets, and their tongues shall dissolve in their mouths.*
> *13 It shall come to pass in that day that a great panic from YHWH will be among them. Everyone will seize the hand of his neighbor, and raise his hand against his neighbor's hand;*

And in addition to gathering up all of the gold, silver and apparel of the Muslim nations that attack Israel, one might imagine that Israel will also take control of whatever oil reserves remain.

> *14 Judah also will fight at Jerusalem. And the wealth of all the surrounding (Islamic) nations shall be gathered together: gold, silver, and apparel in great abundance.*
> *15 Such also shall be the plague on the horse and the mule, on the camel and the donkey, and on all the cattle that will be in those camps. So shall this plague be.*

Then, describing the events *after* the Islamic attacks, Zechariah tells us that everyone who is left of the Muslim nations that came up against Jerusalem will have to go up to Jerusalem year by year to keep the feast, or else they will have no rain. Egypt is even given as an example of one of these Islamic nations.

> **16** And it shall come to pass that everyone who is left of all the (Islamic) nations which came against Jerusalem shall go up from year to year to worship the King, YHWH of hosts, and to keep the Feast of Tabernacles.
> **17** And it shall be that whichever of the families of the earth do not come up to Jerusalem to worship the King, YHWH of hosts, on them there will be no rain.
> **18** If the family of (Islamic) Egypt will not come up and enter in, they shall have no rain; they shall receive the plague with which YHWH strikes the nations who do not come up to keep the Feast of Tabernacles.
> **19** This shall be the punishment of (Islamic) Egypt, and the punishment of all the nations that do not come up to keep the Feast of Tabernacles.

A lot has been said about the 'chem-trails' (a previously secretive U.S. government cloud seeding program). Conspiracy theorists allege that these 'chem-trails' are a satanic plot that Satan is working on, so that those nations who want to defy YHWH can still get rain, even though they will not come up for the Festivals.

It may be that 'chem-trails' are a satanic plot to get around honoring YHWH. However, given the fact that Israel will rule the nations with a rod of iron during the Millennium, Israel may also control any and all cloud-seeding operations that take place. If any nation does not come up to honor YHWH at His Festivals, Israel will still have the power to ensure that they have no rain (just as YHWH's prophecies say).

20 In that day "Set-apartness to YHWH" shall be engraved on the bells of the horses. The pots in YHWH's house shall be like the bowls before the altar.

21 Yes, every pot in Jerusalem and Judah shall be Set-apartness to YHWH of hosts. Everyone who sacrifices shall come and take them and cook in them. In that day there shall no longer be a Canaanite in the House of YHWH of hosts.

The Mark of the Beast

(Note: future editions will also include information about the Islamic 'Bismallah', in addition to this information.)

In the last chapter we saw how the spiritual world is the primary reality, and how the world we live in is a *shadow* of the spiritual realm. We also saw how YHWH forms every *thing* in our world from invisible energies. Interestingly, the Apostle Shaul tells us the same thing. In Hebrews 11:3, he tells us that things which are visible *are not made from* things which can be seen. Let us read the passage closely.

> *Ivrim (Hebrews) 11:3*
> ***3 By faith we understand that the worlds were framed by the word of Elohim, so that the things which are seen were not made of things which are visible.***

Clearly, if the things which can be seen are *not made of* things that can be seen, then these things are made of invisible energies, like we saw in the last chapter. This is in harmony with Scripture, with the eastern view of the world, and with Superstring Theory. But what does it have to say about the Mark of the Beast?

As we already saw (above), the Book of the Revelation is a *vision*, and it is written in symbolic language. While the Book of the Revelation tells us of real events that will take place here on earth, we must remember that Revelation is written entirely in symbolism. When the events finally do take place here on earth, they will probably not look anything like what the vision portrays.

Speaking in symbols, Revelation 13 tells us that there will be a 'beast' that will rise up out of the sea.

> *Gilyana (Revelation) 13:1*
> *13:1 Then I stood on the sand of the sea. And I saw a beast rising up out of the sea, having seven heads and ten horns, and on his horns ten crowns, and on his heads a blasphemous name.*

In *Nazarene Israel*, we showed that the Pope is the anti-Messiah, and that the number of the anti-Messiah's 'name' is 666. (Please see "The Papacy as anti-Messiah," starting on page 66 of *Nazarene Israel*).

As part of that study, we noted that the 'number' of the Beast is *also* the number of a *man* (i.e., the Pope), and his number is 666.

> *Gilyana (Revelation) 13:18*
> *18 Here is wisdom. Let him who has understanding calculate the number of the beast, for it is the number of a man, and his number is 666.*

If the Pope is the anti-Messiah, and if his number of his name is 666, and if the number of the Beast's name is *also* 666, then the Pope (or rather, the Papacy) is the Beast of the Book of the Revelation. However, notice that Revelation *also* tells us that there will be a second beast which will look different than the first. This second beast will make 'all' of the people of the earth worship the first beast (i.e., the Pope, or the Roman Catholic Church).

> *Gilyana (Revelation) 13:11-18*
> *11 Then I saw another beast coming up out of the earth, and he had two horns like a lamb and spoke like a dragon.*
> *12 And he exercises all the authority of the first beast in his presence, and causes the earth and those who dwell in it to worship the first beast, whose deadly wound was healed.*

The Roman Catholic Church received a 'deadly wound' at the time of the Protestant Reformation. However, now the United Nations (which is probably the second beast) is advancing what they call the United Religions Initiative (URI). The United Religions Initiative is the capstone of the Ecumenical Movement (the movement to unite all Christian religions back into one, under the auspices of the Roman Catholic Church).

The United Religions Initiative, however, goes farther than that. The plan is to create one official religion for all people, and to outlaw all other beliefs. Not too surprisingly, this 'United Religion' is to be based on Roman Catholicism, and it is to be formed about the Pope and the Roman Church (which is essentially sun worship dressed up to look like the belief in Yeshua). When the URI is brought into effect, the 'deadly wound' of the Roman Catholic Church will be healed, and an 'image' of the Beast (i.e., the URI) will have been set up for all the people to worship.

> *13 He (second beast) performs great signs, so that he even makes fire come down from heaven on the earth in the sight of men.*

14 And he (second beast) deceives those who dwell on the earth by those signs which he was granted to do in the sight of the (first) beast, telling those who dwell on the earth to make an image to the (first) beast who was wounded by the sword and lived.

15 He (second beast) was granted power to give breath to the image of the beast, that the image of the beast should both speak and cause as many as would not worship the image of the beast to be killed.

16 He (second beast) causes all, both small and great, rich and poor, free and slave, to receive a mark on their right hand or on their foreheads,

17 and that no one may buy or sell except one who has the mark or the name of the (first) beast, or the number of his name.

18 Here is wisdom. Let him who has understanding calculate the number of the (first) beast, for it is the number of a man, and his number is 666.

Notice that the second beast (which is probably the United Nations) will cause all people, small and great, rich and poor, free and slave, to take the mark of the first beast on their right hands, or on their foreheads. Scripture also tells us that whosoever does not take the mark of the first beast will not be able to buy or sell.

However, the next chapter tells us that whoever *does* take the mark of the first beast will be tormented day and night, forever and ever, with fire and brimstone.

> *Gilyana (Revelation) 14:9-11*
> *9 Then a third messenger followed them, saying with a loud voice, "If anyone worships the beast and his image, and receives his mark on his forehead or on his hand,*
> *10 he himself shall also drink of the wine of the wrath of Elohim, which is poured out full strength into the cup of His indignation. He shall be tormented with fire and brimstone in the presence of the set-apart angels and in the presence of the Lamb.*
> *11 And the smoke of their torment ascends forever and ever; and they have no rest day or night, who worship the beast and his image, and whoever receives the mark of his name."*

Let us be wise with regards to how we read Scripture. Revelation 13:16 (above) tells us that the second beast causes 'all' people receive the mark of the first beast on their right hands, or on their foreheads.

> *16 He (second beast) causes all, both small and great, rich and poor, free and slave, to receive a mark on their right hand or on their foreheads,*

Paradoxically, *not* all will receive the Mark of the Beast, because Revelation Chapter Twenty speaks of those who have *not* taken the Mark of the Beast. These will rule and reign with Yeshua's spirit (and with His rod of iron) for a thousand years. These are the Nazarene Israelites.

> *Gilyana (Revelation) 20:4-6*
> *4 And I saw thrones, and they sat on them, and judgment was committed to them. Then I saw the souls of those who had been beheaded for their witness to Yeshua and for the word of Elohim (G-d), who had not worshiped the (first) beast or his image, and had not received his mark on their foreheads or on their hands. And they lived and reigned with Messiah for a thousand years.*
> *5 But the rest of the dead did not live again until the thousand years were finished. This is the first resurrection.*
> *6 Blessed and set-apart is he who has part in the first resurrection. Over such the second death has no power, but they shall be priests of Elohim and of Messiah, and shall reign with Him a thousand years.*

But how can Revelation 13:16 tell us that 'all' will take the Mark of the Beast, and yet Revelation 20 tells us that *not* all will take it? Is Scripture contradicting itself? Elohim forbid! YHWH is just speaking in broad general terms in order to keep the vision 'sealed up' until now.

If we must avoid taking the Mark of the Beast (so that we can rule and reign with Yeshua's spirit, and with His rod of iron), then why not learn what the Mark of the Beast *is*, so we can avoid taking it?

To that end, let us ask a very important question. If the first beast is symbolic of the Pope (and of the Papacy), then what is the *Mark* of the Beast symbolic of?

To ask this question in a different way, if Revelation speaks in symbolic language, then just what exactly does the Mark of the Beast *symbolize*?

Pre-Millennial Return Theory insists there will be a literal, physical Mark of the Beast (which can at least hypothetically be seen with the naked eye). However, the Apostle Shaul tells us that the things that are *seen* are made up of things which are *not visible*.

> **Ivrim (Hebrews) 11:3**
> **3 By faith we understand that the worlds were framed by the word of Elohim, so that the things which are seen were not made of things which are visible.**

If there will be a literal Mark of the Beast (that can be *seen*), then what is it *made of*, in the invisible realm?

In the last chapter we saw that everything that can be seen in the material realm is a *shadow* of something in the spiritual realm. Therefore, if there will be a literal, visible Mark of the Beast, then what does it represent in the *spiritual realm*? That's what we need to know. Otherwise we will focus on the things that can be seen in the material realm, while ignoring the powers and principalities in (invisible) heavenly places.

> **Ephesians 6:12**
> **12 For we do not wrestle against flesh and blood, but against principalities, against powers, against the rulers of the darkness of this age, against spiritual hosts of wickedness in the heavenly places.**

We have already seen that Pre-Millennial Return Theory is in error, because when the Messiah Yeshua returns, the earth and the heavens will be burned up (2nd Peter 3:10-12). However, a quick review of Pre-Millennial Return Theory may be helpful here.

There are many permutations of Pre-Millennial Return Theory. However, according to all versions, the Great Tribulation is supposed to take place at the start of the Millennium (in or around the year 2000). According to most versions, then, during this Great Tribulation, the believers will have to escape persecution by the federal government, which will allegedly try to track them down with squadrons of assault troops in order to put the Mark of the Beast on their right hands or on their foreheads, thus denying them the right to rule and reign with Yeshua (reference Revelation 20:4-6, above).

According to this common pre-millennial scenario, the true believers must avoid taking the Mark of the Beast at any and all costs (even if it means losing their lives), for to take the Mark of the Beast is to lose all possibility of ruling and reigning with a physical Yeshua.

We have already seen that Yeshua cannot return in physical form until the *end* of the Millennium, because both the earth and the heavens will be burned up at Yeshua's second coming (reference 2nd Peter 3:10-12). However, let us look at Pre-Millennial Return Theory's list of candidates for the Mark of the Beast, as it may prove instructive.

Money is always a popular candidate as the Mark of the Beast, since Revelation 13 tells us there will come a time when no one will be able to buy or sell without taking the Mark. (If money is the Mark, then logically, no one can buy or sell without it.)

> *Gilyana (Revelation) 13:16-18*
> **16 He causes all, both small and great, rich and poor, free and slave, to receive a mark on their right hand or on their foreheads,**
> **17 and that no one may buy or sell except one who has the mark or the name of the beast, or the number of his name.**
> **18 Here is wisdom. Let him who has understanding calculate the number of the beast, for it is the number of a man: His number is 666.**

The 'money-Mark' theory points to the satanic imagery all over the U.S. dollar bill, and then suggests that the reason the U.S. dollar is the Mark of the Beast is that at least in America (and at least figuratively speaking), no one can buy or sell without this imagery. That might seem to make sense, except that it is now far more common to buy and sell using debit or credit cards, and chip technology will soon replace those. Further, since the Beast is the Pope and the Papacy is in Rome, how is the *United States* dollar bill the Mark of the Papacy?

Considering that the Euro and the Japanese Yen are fast becoming the world's new currency standards, there are just too many problems with the 'dollar-Mark' hypothesis. Certainly, something is very wrong that satanic imagery exists all over the U.S. dollar bill, but if we accept the 'dollar-Mark' hypothesis, then we are falling into the trap of looking for a *visible* Mark of the Beast, without asking what it *symbolizes*. Since visible things are really only shadows of the true spiritual reality, this really does us no good. Are we to be afraid of a *shadow*?

As cash transactions became less common than debit transactions, focus on the 'dollar-Mark' theory also began to wane. However, new fears arose that the barcode might be the 'new' Mark of the Beast. Since barcodes have a bar with a numerical value of six in the middle, as well as a bar with a numerical value of six on either side, the barcode can be said to have a numerical value of 6-6-6 (so to speak).

There was a time when pretty much no one could buy or sell without either barcodes or cash, but now even the barcode is being phased out in lieu of electronic transponders. These transponders are being inserted into almost all prepackaged goods, so that barcodes will soon be a thing of the past. This gives rise to fears of these electronic transponders being the 'new and improved' Mark of the Beast. However, once again, to focus on a physical object as the Mark of the Beast is to be afraid of a *shadow*, which may make good sense in western logic, but seems completely irrational in an eastern paradigm.

That there are so many satanic images all over the U.S. dollar bill seems like proof-positive that Satan is at work in our world. However, to fear a material *shadow* is to play right into Satan's hands.

There are other things that believers fear as a *material* Mark of the Beast. For example, many now fear the Digital Angel microchip as the Mark. However, to fear any physical object is still to focus on the material realm, instead of focusing the spiritual realm that forms its foundation. YHWH has never been against the use of high-technology devices, or against money. Further, as we will show in *'Migrations: The Lost Ten Tribes,"* YHWH even commands that His people both use and develop high-technology devices.

Satan is the prince of this world, and the reason that so much satanic imagery exists on the back of the U.S. dollar bill is simply because Americans have stopped setting themselves apart. Satanism is the default condition of this world, and unless one takes pains to set oneself apart from it, Satanism will ultimately rule in one's life. Once the American people stopped setting themselves apart from Satan's works of darkness, the satanic imagery crept back in automatically. It was as if one had unplugged a refrigerator, and then wondered why it began to grow mold inside.

This highlights an important point: it is not possible to keep Torah by accident. YHWH gave human beings a default animal nature that longs to fulfill the desires of the flesh. Our bodies crave pleasure. Sin 'crouches by the door,' but our job is to rule over it.

> B'reisheet (Genesis) 4:6-7
> 6 So YHWH said to Cain, "Why are you angry? And why has your countenance fallen?
> 7 If you do well, will it not be lifted up? And if you do not do well, sin crouches by the door. And its desire is for you, but you should rule over it."

America is less set-apart today than ever before, and as America has become slowly less and less set-apart, satanic imagery has crept back into American life, until it is now fairly ubiquitous. As we will see in the next chapter, America is prophesied to be destroyed for the abundance of its many images, and while it is too late to save America, until Ephraim decides to clean himself up spiritually, his external world will reflect the influence and control Satan exerts on his internal one.

Yeshua derided the Pharisees for thinking backwards:

> *Mattai (Matthew) 23:25-28*
> *25 "Woe to you, scribes and Pharisees, hypocrites! For you cleanse the outside of the cup and dish, but inside they are full of extortion and self-indulgence.*
> *26 Blind Pharisee, first cleanse the inside of the cup and dish, that the outside of them may be clean also!*
> *27 "Woe to you, scribes and Pharisees, hypocrites! For you are like whitewashed tombs which indeed appear beautiful outwardly, but inside are full of dead men's bones and all uncleanness.*
> *28 Even so you also outwardly appear righteous to men, but inside you are full of hypocrisy and lawlessness."*

Ironically, Ephraim still shows the same backwards thinking the Pharisees showed back in the first century. While Ephraim's world is tainted with satanic imagery, the root of the problem is not that Ephraim's world has been tainted by the presence of bad symbols. The root of the issue is that Ephraim has failed to set himself apart from Satan's world, and therefore his world cannot help but manifest the satanic images and signs of his (internal) spiritual uncleanness. As Yeshua said, if Ephraim will but cleanse the inside of his cup, then the outside will be cleansed also.

> *26 "Blind Pharisee, first cleanse the inside of the cup and dish, that the outside of them may be clean also!"*

One of Ephraim's challenges is that due to his western mindset, he finds abstract ideas (such as an invisible, spiritual Mark of the Beast) to be much harder to conceptualize than concrete ideas (like a physical mark). While this is certainly understandable, notice the problems that this western mindset causes.

When first learning about the Mark of the Beast, many Ephraimites see the satanic images and signs in the visible world around them, and immediately they begin fearing a visible Mark of the Beast. Since a visible mark *seems* to satisfy the requirement at the p'shat (face value) level, most believers become deluded into believing they understand the Mark, and then they never get past a focus on the physical world. However, this is exactly what Satan wants, because then he has kept Ephraim's focus on the things of the flesh, rather than on the things of YHWH.

How can we combat this tendency in the Ephraimites? It can be very helpful to realize that YHWH works in patterns. YHWH uses the same patterns over and over again, because they work so well for Him. However, this process is not unique to YHWH. Other spirits also work in patterns too, and one of Satan's most common patterns is to provide Israel with visible *substitutes* for the invisible things of the Spirit. The reason Satan continues to use this pattern is simply because it is so very effective. Historically speaking, Israel has always been very easily duped.

For example, in the infamous dialogue between Satan and Havvah (Eve), Satan told Havvah that what Elohim told her was not *surely* true. Then he tempted her with a pleasure that appealed to her eyes, to the lusts of her flesh, and to her sense of pride. That was all it took to get her to begin disobeying His Voice.

> *B'reisheet (Genesis) 3:1-5*
> *3:1 Now the serpent was more cunning than any beast of the field which YHWH Elohim had made. And he said to the woman, "Has Elohim indeed said, 'You shall not eat of every tree of the garden'?"*
> *2 And the woman said to the serpent, "We may eat the fruit of the trees of the garden;*
> *3 but of the fruit of the tree which is in the midst of the garden, Elohim has said, 'You shall not eat it, nor shall you touch it, lest you die.'"*
> *4 Then the serpent said to the woman, "You will not surely die.*
> *5 For Elohim knows that in the day you eat of it your eyes will be opened, and you will be like Elohim, knowing good and evil."*

Then the woman Havvah (who also symbolizes Israel) saw that the fruit of the tree was good for food, that it was pleasant to the eyes, and that it was desirable to make her wise (that is, disobedience to YHWH's Voice promised to give her the wisdom of this world). The visible object appealed to the lusts of her flesh (in this case, taste), to the lusts of her eyes, and to her pride.

> *B'reisheet (Genesis) 3:6*
> *6 So when the woman saw that the tree was good for food, that it was pleasant to the eyes, and a tree desirable to make one wise, she took of its fruit and ate. She also gave to her husband with her, and he ate.*

Since Satan could not convince Havvah that YHWH's words were completely false, he gave her a *substitute* form of obedience to YHWH's commandments which would also allow her to satisfy her lusts in the material world. This is the same pattern that Satan uses today, where he tries to get Israel to believe in some form of a visible *substitute* for the Mark of the Beast.

Satan's acts of substitution, however, do not stop there. One of the most flagrant examples of substitution is how Satan got our forefathers to worship a *visible* image, instead of worshipping the *invisible* Elohim.

> **Shemote (Exodus) 32:2-4**
> **2 And Aharon said to them, "Break off the golden earrings which are in the ears of your wives, your sons, and your daughters, and bring them to me."**
> **3 So all the people broke off the golden earrings which were in their ears, and brought them to Aaron.**
> **4 And he received the gold from their hand, and he fashioned it with an engraving tool, and made a molded calf.**
> **Then they said, "This is your god, O Israel, that brought you out of the land of Egypt!"**

The spirit is willing, but the flesh is weak. Rather than walk by faith, we prefer to walk by sight. We love visible *substitutes* for the truth because it is easier to focus on *visible* things. Rather than trust an *invisible* Elohim, we prefer to put our trust in something we can see (even if our own right hand has made it).

> *Melachim Aleph (1ˢᵗ Kings) 12:28-33*
> *28 Therefore the king asked advice, made two calves of gold, and said to the people, "It is too much for you to go up to Jerusalem. Here are your elohim (g-ds), O Israel, which brought you up from the land of Egypt!"*
> *29 And he set up one in Bethel, and the other he put in Dan.*
> *30 Now this thing became a sin, for the people went to worship before the one as far as Dan.*
> *31 He made shrines on the high places, and made priests from every class of people, who were not of the sons of Levi.*

We Ephraimites just never seem to learn. Apart from making 'eye dolls' (idols) to worship, we also like to adopt satanic substitutes for the festival days.

As we explain in *Nazarene Israel*, our evil ancestor King Jeroboam substituted *other* festival days for the ones that YHWH had commanded. Thus Jeroboam set the precedent for Ephraim's spiritual descendants (the Christians) to worship on the (substitute) pagan festival days of Christmas and Easter.

> *32 Jeroboam ordained a feast on the fifteenth day of the eighth month, like the feast that was in Judah, and offered sacrifices on the altar. So he did at Bethel, sacrificing to the calves that he had made. And at Bethel he installed the priests of the high places which he had made.*

> *33 So he made offerings on the altar which he had made at Bethel on the fifteenth day of the eighth month, in the month which he had devised in his own heart. And he ordained a feast for the children of Israel, and offered sacrifices on the altar and burned incense.*

We will talk about what the Mark of the Beast really is in a little while, but notice that the pattern here continues to be one of *substitution*. If Satan cannot get us to *deny* our faith, then at least he wants to get us to adopt a *substitute* form of the worship (as this still causes us to miss the mark, and therefore we still fail to earn an eternal reward).

Satan wants to get Israel to fear a visible *substitute* for the *invisible* (spiritual) Mark of the Beast, because that way, Israel will still be expending mental and spiritual energy in the wrong direction (which will still keep the Israelites from earning an eternal reward).

Why is Satan so successful in getting Israel to focus on *visible* substitutes? Could it be that our flesh inherently desires to run after the lusts of the *eyes*, the lusts of the *flesh*, and the pride of our lives?

> *Yochanan Aleph (1st John) 2:16-17*
> *16 For all that is in the world — the lust of the flesh, the lust of the eyes, and the pride of life — is not of the Father but is of the world.*
> *17 And the world is passing away, and the lust of it; but he who does the will of Elohim abides forever.*

Believers are easily led away from a focus on the invisible things of YHWH, in favor of the material things of Satan (that can be seen, or felt, or enjoyed). This exact same principle (of humans turning away from the invisible, in favor of the visible) is what brought about the downfall of Adam and Havvah (Eve).

> ***B'reisheet (Genesis) 3:6***
> ***6 So when the woman saw that the tree was good for food, that it was pleasant to the eyes, and a tree desirable to make one wise, she took of its fruit and ate. She also gave to her husband with her, and he ate.***

We are easily enticed by the lusts of our eyes, the lusts of our flesh, and the pride of our lives. We are easily led astray from spiritual things (and from Elohim's commandments) by the pleasures of the flesh, whether those pleasures are carnal, sensual, visual, tactile, or what-have-you. Our flesh longs to crave pleasures.

However, notice that when Kepha (Peter) took his eyes off Yeshua, he began to sink. This is also allegorical. When Kepha took his focus off of the Spirit (to focus on the things of the material realm) he more or less 'fell from grace' (and could no longer walk on water).

> ***Mattai (Matthew) 14:28-30***
> ***28 And Kepha answered Him and said, "Master, if it is You, command me to come to You on the water."***
> ***29 So He said, "Come." And when Kepha had come down out of the boat, he walked on the water to go to Yeshua.***

> **30 But when he saw that the wind was boisterous, he was afraid; and beginning to sink he cried out, saying, "Master, save me!"**

This same concept applies to hearing and obeying His Voice. When we allow ourselves to be distracted from that sense of inner stillness and calm in which His voice can be heard, we fall out of His favor (grace).

The world is filled with distractions, and Satan loves to distract us. Opportunity may knock, but temptation leans on the buzzer. Satan wants to destroy our focus on invisible spiritual things by any and all means possible, and he knows that we are predisposed to fear a visible, *physical* Mark of the Beast.

Yet some pre-millennialists still claim that the World Wide Web is the Mark of the Beast, in that the letter 'w' equates to the Hebrew letter Vav (ו), which has a numerical value of six (and thus w-w-w equals ו-ו-ו, or 6-6-6). But is the Internet a part of the Roman Catholic Church, that use of the Internet is a Mark of the Pope? And how do the pre-millennialists explain the fact that Nazarene movement was made possible (at least in part) by the development of the Internet?

Many Ephraimites believe that just so long as they do not use dollar bills, or purchase anything with a barcode off the Internet, or that so long as no one puts an electronic microchip in their hands, that they can refuse to die to the flesh, and still be spiritually pure. When will Ephraim learn that he cannot become spiritually pure just by avoiding the outward physical *manifestations* of spiritual allegiance to Satan? When will he learn about spiritual things?

When will Ephraim learn that the Mark of the Beast is allegiance to the Beast, and that the Mark of YHWH is allegiance (including full obedience) to YHWH?

While Revelation does speak of a Mark of the Beast, Revelation 7 tells us that the *bondservants of Elohim* will also receive a 'seal' on their foreheads before the earth is harmed.

> ***Gilyana (Revelation) 7:3***
> ***3 Saying, "Do not harm the earth, the sea, or the trees till we have sealed the servants of our Elohim on their foreheads."***

The pre-millennialists insist that the Mark of the Beast is supposed to be a visible mark. However, if that were true, then should we not expect that the seal which will be placed on the foreheads of the servants of Elohim will also be physical?

But has anyone ever heard the pre-millennialists argue that the seal on the foreheads of the servants of Elohim will be a physical seal? The idea is laughable, because the 'seal' is not a reference to a visible mark, but a reference to Elohim's favor ('grace').

Scripture tells us it is an abomination to use unequal weights and measures.

> ***Devarim (Deuteronomy) 25:13-16***
> ***13 "You shall not have in your bag differing weights, a heavy and a light.***
> ***14 You shall not have in your house differing measures, a large and a small.***

**15 You shall have a perfect and just weight, a perfect and just measure, that your days may be lengthened in the land which YHWH your Elohim is giving you.
16 For all who do such things, all who behave unrighteously, are an abomination to YHWH your Elohim.**

Why, then, does Pre-Millennial Return Theory teach us to look for a *physical* Mark of the Beast, but not to look for a *physical* seal on the foreheads of the servants of Elohim? Are they not using unequal weights and measures?

How curious that the pre-millennialists should spend all of their time worried about how not to take the Mark of the Beast! If there is a Mark of the Beast, then does it not also stand to reason that there is a Mark of YHWH? And if there is a Mark of YHWH, then would it not be infinitely wiser to spend one's time praying about how to make sure that one has YHWH's mark?

In addition to Revelation 7, Ezekiel 9 speaks of a mark that will be put on the foreheads of those who sigh and cry over all of the abominations that are done in Jerusalem. These are then given a 'mark' that spares them from the coming destruction on the hypocrites.

The word that is used in Ezekiel 9 to describe the 'mark' that is put on the foreheads of those who love YHWH is the Hebrew word 'Tav' (תָו).

> *OT:8420 tav (tawv); from OT:8427; a mark; by implication, a signature:*
> *KJV - desire, mark.*

Let us read about how this mark (תָו) is given.

> *Yehezqel (Ezekiel) 9:1-7*
> *1 Then He called out in my hearing with a loud voice, saying, "Let those who have charge over the city draw near, each with a deadly weapon in his hand."*
> *2 And suddenly six men came from the direction of the upper gate, which faces north, each with his battle-ax in his hand. One man among them was clothed with linen and had a writer's inkhorn at his side. They went in and stood beside the bronze altar.*
> *3 Now the glory of the Elohim of Israel had gone up from the cherub, where it had been, to the threshold of the temple. And He called to the man clothed with linen, who had the writer's inkhorn at his side;*
> *4 and YHWH said to him, "Go through the midst of the city, through the midst of Jerusalem, and put a mark (תָו) on the foreheads of the men who sigh and cry over all the abominations that are done within it."*
> *5 To the others He said in my hearing, "Go after him through the city and kill; do not let your eye spare, nor have any pity.*
> *6 Utterly slay old and young men, maidens and little children and women; but do not come near anyone on whom is the mark (תָו); and begin at My sanctuary." So they began with the elders who were before the temple.*

> **7** Then He said to them, "Defile the temple, and fill the courts with the slain. Go out!" And they went out and killed in the city.

Like Revelation, this portion of Ezekiel is a vision, and it speaks in symbolic language. It describes a time when *many* worshippers will stand near to YHWH's Temple (spiritually speaking); but that these will be slain because they are hypocrites. They are not truly allegiant to YHWH. Only those who are truly allegiant to YHWH are given the mark that YHWH has commanded be put on the forehead of all those who sigh and cry over all the abominations that are done in Jerusalem.

However, since this is a *vision*, should we expect to see six armed men physically slaying the millions who do not receive a visible, *literal* mark on their foreheads from a man with a literal writer's inkhorn? Or (since this is a vision) should we understand that destruction will fall upon those who do not receive YHWH's *spiritual* mark on their foreheads (because they did not demonstrate their allegiance and obedience to Him)?

Remembering that the Israelite faith is an eastern one, and that in eastern thought it is understood that visible things are symbolic of things in the spiritual world, then when Scripture speaks of a 'mark' on one's forehead, is this a reference to a *visible* mark? Or is it not rather a reference to a *spiritual* mark?

And if it is a reference to a spiritual mark, then what kind of a spiritual mark is it? Could it be symbolic of everything that one thinks? Or could it be symbolic of one's allegiance?

Should the faithful expect to be branded? Or should the faithful expect to receive a tattoo from YHWH on their foreheads? The idea is almost funny, because the mindset is so limited that it tries to force an invisible Elohim to operate exclusively in the visible world.

The second word that YHWH uses to describe the mark on His people is the Hebrew word 'oht' (אוֹת).

> *OT:226 'owt (אוֹת); probably from OT:225 (in the sense of appearing); a signal (literally or figuratively), as a flag, beacon, monument, omen, prodigy, evidence, etc.:*
>
> *KJV - mark, miracle, (en-) sign, token.*

While the word תָו is more like a signature, the word אוֹת describes an outward manifestation of an inward condition. It is a mark or a sign in the sense of being a *reflection* of one's inward spiritual condition.

The word אוֹת is used in the Great Shema, which Yeshua said was the first and the greatest of all the commandments (reference Matthew 22:35-38). The Great Shema commands all who would be Israelites to bind YHWH's words on their foreheads and on their right hands as a *sign* (or as a *mark*) of their devotion, allegiance and obedience to Him.

> *Devarim (Deuteronomy) 6:4-9*
> *4 "Hear, O Israel: YHWH our Elohim, YHWH is one!*
> *5 You shall love YHWH your Elohim with all your heart, with all your soul, and with all your strength.*

6 And these words which I command you today shall be in your heart.
7 You shall teach them diligently to your children, and shall talk of them when you sit in your house, when you walk by the way, when you lie down, and when you rise up.
8 You shall bind them as a sign (אוֹת) on your hand, and they shall be as frontlets between your eyes.
9 You shall write them on the doorposts of your house and on your gates.

Perhaps one reason Yeshua said the Great Shema is the greatest of all the commandments is that if Israel would truly keep this commandment, then Israel would keep all of the others as well, for the word 'shema' means not just to hear, but to hear with the intent to obey. Basically, it means to hear and obey His Voice.

> **OT:8085 shama` (shaw-mah'); a primitive root; to hear intelligently (often with implication of attention, obedience, etc.; causatively, to tell, etc.):**

Let us take a look at verse 8 in the Hebrew.

8 You shall bind them as a sign on your hand, and they shall be as frontlets between your eyes.	(8) וּקְשַׁרְתָּם לְאוֹת עַל יָדֶךָ ׀ וְהָיוּ לְטֹטָפֹת בֵּין עֵינֶיךָ

Scripture is not just one-dimensional. It has many layers of meaning, and at multiple levels. One of the technical requirements of verse 8, then, is the command to bind His Words as a *sign* on our right hands, and on our foreheads. While most western Christians interpret this only in a spiritual sense (i.e., to think about his words a lot), Judah interprets this command both literally *and* spiritually.

In addition to binding His words on their hearts, Judah also binds a thing called 'tefillin' (phylacteries) on their right hands and on their foreheads. They bind these tefillin as a visible *sign* (אות) of their inward devotion toward Elohim.

Since no one binds tefillin unless they want to obey YHWH's Word, the act of binding tefillin serves as an outward *sign* (or an outward *mark*) of one's devotion to YHWH. In this, it is in the same class of signs as, the Sabbath, Passover and physical circumcision. People only do these things out of a desire to serve Elohim.

However, just as with physical circumcision, there is also a fine point of distinction to be made with regards to tefillin (or the Sabbath, or any of the commands). Shaul tells us that physical circumcision is nothing, in and of itself. Rather, what is important is that one is doing one's best to guard YHWH's commandments.

> *Qorintim Aleph (1st Corinthians) 7:19*
> *19 Circumcision is nothing, and uncircumcision is nothing; but the keeping of the commandments of Elohim (is what matters).*

What matters is that we do our best to obey His Torah.

The Mark of YHWH, then, is our total allegiance and obedience to YHWH, even unto the point of death. But notice something else: even though Yeshua probably was not wearing tefillin at His torture at Golgotha, He certainly had YHWH's mark. That is, His actions were actions of loyalty and allegiance to YHWH. His actions were actions of obedience, even unto a terrible, painful death on the cross.

> **Philippim (Philippians) 2:5-8**
> **5 Let this mind be in you which was also in Messiah Yeshua,**
> **6 who, being in the form of Elohim, did not consider it robbery to be equal with Elohim,**
> **7 but made Himself of no reputation, taking the form of a bondservant, and coming in the likeness of men.**
> **8 And being found in appearance as a man, He humbled Himself and became obedient to the point of death, even the death of the cross.**

Even if the visible outward physical signs of allegiance (in this case, tefillin) were not present at the moment of Yeshua's death, does this detract anything from the depth of His dedication and servitude unto YHWH?

This point is confusing to many in Ephraim who still have a western mindset. They tend to fear a physical Mark of the Beast, and even though they stop short of keeping all of His commandments, when they do not see a visible mark on their right hand or on their forehead, they assume that they have not taken the Mark of the Beast. They feel there is no problem even though they neither hear nor obey His Voice.

Just because we might be physically circumcised, bind tefillin, and keep the Sabbath and festival days, does that mean that our hearts are upright before YHWH? The Pharisees were all physically circumcised, bound tefillin, and kept both the Sabbath and festival days zealously, and yet Yeshua did not seem to think that they were particularly righteous.

> **Mattai (Matthew) 23:27-28**
> **27 "Woe unto you, scribes and Pharisees, hypocrites! For you are like whitewashed tombs which indeed appear beautiful outwardly, but inside are full of dead men's bones and all uncleanness.**
> **28 Even so you also outwardly appear righteous to men, but inside you are full of hypocrisy and Torahlessness!"**

Here is another thought that many might find difficult. If the performance of these four external *signs* (אֹתֹת) of our love for YHWH do not necessarily indicate that we really love and serve YHWH, then why would the presence or absence of a physical microchip indicate allegiance to Satan?

Just for the sake of argument, let us suppose the pre-millennial hypothesis is right, and the believers will all be implanted with physical microchips: does that mean that none of us will make it into the Kingdom?

And should we not take jobs, or hold down employment just because we might be paid in U.S. dollars? And will we lose all chance of receiving eternal salvation if we purchase something on the Internet? Or are we defiled if we own something with a barcode on it?

And if handling strange currency causes one to lose one's salvation, then where does that leave Yeshua? Yeshua grew up under the Roman system, and when He received His gift of gold, frankincense and myrrh, it was probably of Babylonian coinage (i.e., Babylonian tribute). Did Yeshua lose His eternal salvation, just because Joseph and Miriam may have once handled coinage while in Egypt?

And what is the root of the great fear over the Digital Angel microchip? As disgusting as the thought of taking electronic circuitry under our skin is, 'the Chip' is simply a technological innovation that promises to make commerce easier. Much like debit cards, and much like cash that went before that, it is simply an easier way to do business.

We have already seen that Scripture tells us there will be persecution in the days and years ahead. The problem with the 'Chip-Mark' theory, however, is that the 'Chip-Mark' theorists ask us to turn our attentions *away* from the spiritual realm, and put our attention on the visible, material realm. As we have already seen, this is precisely what Satan wants, because it takes our focus off of the spiritual realm.

Let us suppose that the United States government does suspend the Constitution and declare martial law, as is authorized under Presidential Executive Order #12919. Suppose there is a 'lesser tribulation' of sorts before the House of Ephraim is regathered to the Land of Israel. Let us further suppose that you and I will be forced into the concentration camps that the U.S. Federal Emergency Management Administration has already built, and that we are then forcibly implanted with Digital Angel microchips. Why would that cause us to lose our eternal salvation?

At least according to standard pre-millennial thought, the purpose of declaring martial law is so that the U.S. Government can then hunt down all those believers who have refused to take 'the chip,' even using the latest in military satellite technology to direct squadrons of helicopter assault troops to track those true believers down in the wilderness. Once taken captive they will then be chained, and forcibly implanted with a Digital Angel Corporation microchips, thus bringing to a tragic end all possibility of their quest to live next to Yeshua.

What kind of strange doctrine is this? Since when did having something forcibly implanted into our hands cause us to lose our position in the Kingdom? Yeshua had huge spikes forcibly thrust through His hands by the Romans. Did that take away His eternal salvation?

Is the use of high-technology prohibited, in Scripture? And how could it possibly destroy our eternal salvation to have something forcibly implanted into our bodies against our own will? What sense does that make?

And did Yeshua not plainly tell us **not** to fear those who could destroy only the body, but not kill the soul?

> **Mattai (Matthew) 10:28**
> **28 And do not fear those who kill the body, but cannot kill the soul. But rather, fear Him who is able to destroy both soul and body in hell.**

Can we see that the pre-millennialists have fallen prey to Satan's plan to deceive us, by getting Israel to focus on a visible, material *substitute* for His mark? Satan has them focused on the *signs* of Satan's reign, but nothing that indicates *allegiance* to him.

The Mark of YHWH is that we lay down our lives, and seek to obey His Voice in all things. In other words, we obtain the Mark of YHWH because of our unswerving obedience to Him, even unto the point of death.

The Mark of the Beast, on the other hand, comes to us simply because we fail to serve YHWH unswervingly. Like our earlier example of the refrigerator, if we stop making the refrigerator cold (or if we stop adding wood to the sacrificial fire), everything becomes lukewarm.

Is everything that we *think* oriented towards serving YHWH? Do we love YHWH with *all* our mind? If so, then we already have YHWH's mark on our forehead.

Is everything that we *do* focused on serving YHWH? Do we consciously work at being a good witness for Him as we live in the world (and yet are not of it)? Are we doing all we can to help build the Stick of Ephraim, so that prophecy can be fulfilled, and YHWH's Kingdom on earth can be restored? If so, then we already have YHWH's mark on our right hand.

However, if allegiance to YHWH (to include keeping all of His commandments even unto the death) is the 'Mark of YHWH,' then what is the 'Mark of the Beast?'

Remembering that the Beast is the Pope (and the Papacy), the Mark of the Beast would be *allegiance* to the Pope, and to his commandments and festival days. In Scriptural terms, to keep the Pope's commandments would be to pledge allegiance to the Pope, for it was the Pope who first told the believers to keep the pagan festival days. This mark would apply not only to the Roman Catholic Church, but also to the Protestant churches, most of which keep at least some of the same festival days.

If you pledge allegiance to YHWH Elohim, and if literally everything that you think, and everything that you do is oriented towards serving Him, then spiritually speaking, you may already have His mark on your right hand, and on your forehead. If you diligently seek to keep *all* of His commandments (and not just the ones that you like), then you are probably already 'marked' as being one of His.

And, conversely, if you do not joyfully obey the whole of the Torah, and if everything you do is *not* already oriented towards building His Son's empire, then you probably do not have the Mark of YHWH. If so, then the time to rededicate yourself to building His Kingdom is now, for today is the acceptable day of salvation.

> *Qorintim Bet (2nd Corinthians) 6:1-2*
> *1 We then, as workers together with Him also plead with you not to receive the favor (grace) of Elohim in vain.*
> *2 For He says:*
> *"In an acceptable time I have heard you, and in the day of salvation I have helped you."*
>
> *Behold: now is the accepted time!*
> *Behold: now is the day of salvation.*

America: Daughter of Babylon

(Note: Future editions will include additional information about an Islamic 'Daughter of Babylon as well.)

Israel has been a *family* right from the start, and Judah still generally understands that each Jew is responsible for health and welfare of every other Jew.

> ***B'reisheet (Genesis) 4:9***
> ***9 Then YHWH said to Cain, "Where is Abel your brother?"***
> ***He said, "I do not know. Am I my brother's keeper?"***

However, while Israel is a *family*, and while all Israelites are related to each other (and are responsible for one another), America knows no such requirement. Rather, America claims to be a collection of individual families, whose only joint goal is the pursuit of life, liberty, happiness and individual freedom.

There may have been neighborhood and community feeling in America (and in other parts of the West) before the Cultural Revolution of the 1960's. However, with the demise of the Christian ethic in western society and the Ten Commandments being removed from the schools, America has transformed from being a melting pot, to something more like a cultural fruit salad.

While metal alloys that are melted together in a pot can be strong and long lived, fruit salads are never long lived. And, while steel can be used to build something enduring (for the future) the fate of a fruit salad is either to be consumed, or to spoil.

If YHWH wills, we will talk more about how to reorient ourselves away from western individualism to Hebraic familial unity in *'Building the Stick.'* However, in this chapter we will see why America is the 'daughter of Babylon,' and why she will be destroyed for her selfish individualistic attitudes of 'liberty' and 'freedom.'

Many Christian Constitutionalists are continually up in arms over the erosions of their personal freedoms and rights. One wonders if they realize that such personal freedoms and rights are granted nowhere in Scripture, and for them to protest for them plays right into the hands of the satanic secret societies of the Illuminati and the Masonic Lodge.

Legend has it that America's Founding Fathers were Christian men who wrote the Constitution by thumbing back and forth between Leviticus and Deuteronomy, hoping to create a document that could guide a New Covenant people into a better way of life. Aside from the fact that many of the Founding Fathers were Masons, even if this legend were true, we should be careful to note that an attempt to create a document *apart* from Scripture, referencing only a *subset* of Scripture, does not equal governance *by* Scripture. Further, we should note that the Constitution actually gives a form of government that is almost diametrically opposed to the kingship that Scripture advocates.

Constitutionalists argue that Scripture does not call for Israel to have a king. This argument is based on their misunderstanding of one passage in First Samuel.

> *Shemuel Aleph (1st Samuel) 8:4-5*
> *4 Then all the elders of Israel gathered together and came to Shemu'el at Ramah,*

> *5 and said to him, "Look, you are old, and your sons do not walk in your ways. Now make us a king to judge us like all the nations."*

It was not Israel's desire for a king that upset Shemuel, for YHWH had already told Israel that they *would* have a king. However, Israel was not supposed to desire a king who was *like the kings of the other nations*.

> *Devarim (Deuteronomy) 17:14-15*
> *14 "When you come to the land which YHWH your Elohim is giving you, and possess it and dwell in it, and say, 'I will set a king over me like all the nations that are around me,'*
> *15 you shall surely set a king over you whom YHWH your Elohim chooses. One from among your brethren you shall set as king over you. You may not set a foreigner over you, who is not your brother.*

Israel's sin was not in asking for a king, for YHWH had already told Israel that they would have one. Rather, Israel's sin was in asking *Shemuel* to appoint a king for them, and also in asking for a king like all the *other* nations. That is, the Israelites did not want *YHWH* to appoint them a set-apart king.

> *Shemuel Aleph (1st Samuel) 8:19-20*
> *19 Nevertheless the people refused to obey the voice of Shemuel; and they said, "No, but we will have a king over us,*

> *20 that we also may be like all the nations, and that our king may judge us and go out before us and fight our battles."*

Israel's sin was not in wanting a king. Israel's sin was in not wanting to be ruled by a king *of YHWH's choice*. Israel wanted Samuel to appoint a king of their choice. YHWH considered that in rejecting the king of His choice, Israel was rejecting *Him*.

> *Shemuel Aleph (1st Samuel) 8:7*
> *7 And YHWH said to Shemuel, "Heed the voice of the people in all that they say to you; for they have not rejected you, but they have rejected Me, that I should not reign over them.*
> *8 According to all the works which they have done since the day that I brought them up out of Egypt, even to this day — with which they have forsaken Me and served other gods — so they are doing to you also.*

Like errant school children, Israel did not want to be a special people set-apart unto YHWH. They wanted to be like all of the other nations around them. They wanted to fit in with their peers, and be cool. YHWH considered this tantamount to rebellion against Him.

> *Shemuel Aleph (1st Samuel) 8:9*
> *9 Now therefore, heed their voice. However, you shall solemnly forewarn them, and show them the behavior of the king who will reign over them."*

Shemuel then told the people that there would come a day when they would cry out to YHWH for help from the king they asked for, but that YHWH would not hear them in that day.

> **Shemuel Aleph (1st Samuel) 8:18**
> **18 And you will cry out in that day because of your king whom you have chosen for yourselves, but YHWH will not hear you in that day."**

Nevertheless, Israel refused to hear Shemuel's words of warning, and again told Shemuel that they wanted him to appoint a king over them, so that they could be like all of the other nations.

> **Shemuel Aleph (1st Samuel) 8:19-20**
> **19 Nevertheless the people refused to obey the voice of Shemuel; and they said, "No, but we will have a king over us,**
> **20 that we also may be like all the nations, and that our king may judge us and go out before us and fight our battles."**

Ironically, America's Christian Constitutionalists are crying out to YHWH for help from their government even now. They are asking Him to give them a return to a constitutional form of government, and they do not understand why YHWH does not answer them, despite the fact that Scripture never advocates a 'Constitution,' and in spite of the fact that rule by democracy is essentially a repeat effort by Ephraim to set a king over himself.

Many Christians believe democracy to be superior to kingship, when Scripture never advocates democracy. In fact, Deuteronomy 17:14-15 clearly states that Israel was supposed to have a king (of YHWH's choosing); and yet many Christians believe that it would have been better for Israel never to have had a king. This is ironic, considering the fact that Yeshua is a King.

> *Gilyana (Revelation) 17:14*
> *14 These will make war with the Lamb, and the Lamb will overcome them, for He is Master of masters and King of kings; and those who are with Him are called, chosen, and faithful."*

Even though YHWH wants Israel to have a king of His choosing, many Christian Constitutionalists despise the thought of having a kingship. Instead, they desire a complete return to the vast personal freedoms found in the early days of the American Republic. This is very sad, for as we will see, such freedoms are Babylonian in nature. Unbridled, unfocused freedom is actually a key factor leading to America's coming downfall. But why would America's freedom lead to her downfall?

The Apostle Ya'akov tells us that no one can have true peace (Shalom) unless his theology is first pure.

> *Ya'akov (James) 3:13-17*
> *13 Who is wise and understanding among you? Let him show by good conduct that his works are done in the meekness of wisdom.*
> *14 But if you have bitter envy and self-seeking in your hearts, do not boast and lie against the truth.*

> **15** This wisdom does not descend from above, but is earthly, sensual, demonic.
> **16** For where envy and self-seeking exist, confusion and every evil thing are there.
> **17** But the wisdom that is from above is <u>first</u> pure, <u>then</u> peaceable, gentle, willing to yield, full of mercy and good fruits, without partiality and without hypocrisy.

Before something can be at peace, first it must be pure. Where envy and self-seeking exist, there is confusion and every evil thing. But what is an unbridled free-market 'meritocracy' such as America, if not a forum for envy and self-seeking (self-interest)? And how can this lead to longevity, or lasting internal peace?

Scripture is not against capitalism, but in Scripture, the people are supposed to look out for their brothers (this is the whole function of the third tithe). This stands in contrast to the electoral process established by the Founding Fathers, in which the average man votes his own self interest (or the self interest of his group). Thus the freedom to serve self becomes freedom *from* YHWH, and freedom *from* responsibility to brethren. Is there some reason for YHWH to bless this?

The Founding Fathers clearly understood that free-market capitalism could only produce good so long as the American people believed in YHWH, and obeyed Scripture: that much is clear from their writings. However, rather than found the new republic upon one single theology that was *first pure*, they set a precedent for religious pluralism.

As we will see as this chapter progresses, religious pluralism is the quintessence of the Babylonian spirit, and America is known in prophecy as the 'daughter of Babylon.' Scripture tells us that the ultimate fate of the daughter of Babylon is to be destroyed.

And why should it not be destroyed? America has served YHWH well as a temporary resting stop for the Ephraimite people, while He went to give them rest.

> *Yirmeyahu (Jeremiah) 31:1-2*
> *2 Thus says YHWH: "The people who survived the sword found favor in the wilderness — Israel, when I went to give him rest."*

And yet, while YHWH brought His bride Ephraim into the temporary resting place called 'America,' He also intends to bring her into the Valley of Achor (the Valley of Troubles), that in our troubles with Islam, we might turn to Him once again with our whole hearts, and serve Him as one man, as we did in the days YHWH brought us up from the Land of Egypt. He is bringing Ephraim into the Valley of Troubles, so that she might learn to pull together as His people once again.

> *Hosea 2:14-15*
> *14 'Therefore, behold, I will allure her, will bring her into the wilderness, and speak comfort to her.*
> *15 I will give her her vineyards from there, and the Valley of Troubles as a door of hope. She shall sing there, as in the days of her youth, as in the day when she came up from the land of Egypt.*

But when the Apostle Ya'akov tells us that only confusion and evil come from self-seeking and envy, then what is the future of American democracy, in a world where YHWH gives people enough rope to hang themselves? And what will become of Ephraim, who presently values his freedom and independence more than he values the opportunity to serve YHWH as one man?

In the Septuagint (the Greek LXX), the word 'holocaust' means a 'burnt offering.'

> **Vayiqra (Leviticus) 1:4**
> **4 Then he shall put his hand on the head of the burnt offering (holocaust), and it will be accepted on his behalf to make atonement for him.**

Judah suffered the 'Great Holocaust' prior to being brought back to the Land of Israel. Fully one-third of world Jewry died, and yet the Great Holocaust was not the Great Tribulation, but only a (relatively) minor tribulation.

What was the purpose of the Great Holocaust, if it was not the Great Tribulation? Simply this: like Ephraim, the Jews had become accustomed to living outside of the Land of Israel, and they had become comfortable out in the world. That is, they had become comfortable in 'Babylon.' YHWH had to give Judah some strong medicine, in order to get him to want to leave the world and its Babylonian (and Egyptian) systems behind, and return back home to His land.

But if Judah had to suffer tribulation before he was ready to leave Babylon, then what of Ephraim?

Satan is working hard to build a secular one world government, to be headed by the United Nations. Actually, it could be said that the United Nations is already a satanic one world government: only, it is not yet brought to full power. However, just by reading the daily news, we can easily see how Satan and his minions are diligently striving to bring this secular one world government to full power, and soon.

However, what is the Scriptural purpose of this secular one world government? It is probably something that has happened before, since King Solomon tells us that there is nothing new under the sun.

> ***Qohelet (Ecclesiastes) 1:9***
> ***9 That which has been is what will be. That which is done is what will be done, and there is nothing new under the sun.***

If one wants to know what YHWH is *going* to do, many times all one has to do is to look at what YHWH has *already* done. So was there ever any *other* attempt at forging a secular world government of men, such that men felt they would not have to serve Elohim?

Genesis 11:4 tells us that after the Flood, some of the people (who lived in modern-day Iraq) conspired to build a city whose tower reached unto the heavens.

> ***B'reshit (Genesis) 11:4***
> ***4 And they said, "Come, let us build us a city, and a tower whose top (may reach) unto heaven, and let us make us a name, lest we be scattered abroad upon the face of the whole earth."***

Commentators suggest various motivations for wanting to build the Tower of Babylon, ranging from not having to worry about another Flood, to a desire to actively wage war against Elohim. However, one thing seems certain: the purpose of building the tower (and the city) was not to worship and serve Elohim, but to *get around* worshipping and serving Elohim.

If we have eyes to see, there are parallels to America. America hosts (and subsidizes) the United Nations, which is a world governing body that seeks to unite all of the many nations of the world: but without Elohim. The United Nations exists in a towering building, and it is working to establish a secular New World Order that does not want to worship or serve Elohim.

We will see other parallels between America and the Babylon of Scripture. However, to see them, let us take a quick look at history.

When the Exile to Babylon was over (in 457 BCE), only ten percent of the Jews came back to the Land of Israel. Why did so few Jews want to come back home? Before we judge, let us consider some facts.

While it is a great joy to worship and serve YHWH, His service is intended to be difficult. If it was easy to serve YHWH, then how would He know who truly loved Him (and who did not)? How would He know whom to take for His bride, if the worship was easy?

In comparison to life in Israel, life in Babylon was soft, and easy. The tithes were not enforced, and the Babylonian government did not care if the people kept Torah. The economy in Babylon was relatively strong, and those in the Exile enjoyed the protection of the finest military of their day (just as in America).

In contrast, the Land of Israel was left desolate from the earlier war with Babylon, and marauding bands of raiders (similar to terrorists, in a sense) still ran amok. If we think about it, the decision the Jews faced at the end of the Babylonian Exile was very similar to the decision the Jews would face over two thousand years later, under the Balfour Declaration.

When it was established in 1917, the (mainly British) Balfour Declaration encouraged Jews the world over to return back to their ancestral homeland. However, while many Russian Jews chose to relocate (as Russia's economy was then in shambles), not as many American or European Jews chose to return back home. There were many reasons for this, and there were limits placed on immigration from America and Europe. However, because the economic conditions in Europe and America were superior to those in Israel, many found it easier simply to stay out in the world than to return on back home, because the economic standards were so much better out in 'Babylon.'

The picture is complex, but if it took the Holocaust to convince most Jews of the need to leave the material wealth and prosperity of the west and return back to YHWH's land, then how will things go for Ephraim? Where is his heart, really?

Ephraim likes to believe he will never suffer the same kinds of trials as Judah, because he has Yeshua. He also likes to believe he is special because of his short happy history in the ex-British colonies of America, New Zealand, Australia, South Africa, and the rest of the old British Empire. However, Scripture foretells great tribulation on Ephraim (e.g., Hosea 2:14-15, above), and as we saw earlier, Ishmael is prophesied to 'bitterly grieve' Ephraim (e.g., Genesis 49:23).

The apostles all suffered tribulation, and Yeshua told us that we will suffer tribulation in this world, if we are really His.

> **Yochanan (John) 15:18-21**
> **18 "If the world hates you, you know that it hated Me before it hated you.**
> **19 If you were of the world, the world would love its own. Yet because you are not of the world, but I chose you out of the world, therefore the world hates you.**
> **20 Remember the word that I said to you, 'A servant is not greater than his master.' If they persecuted Me, they will also persecute you. If they kept My word, they will keep yours also.**
> **21 But all these things they will do to you for My name's sake, because they do not know Him who sent Me.**

Acts 10:34 tells us that YHWH is not a respecter of persons, and if Judah had to suffer tribulation before he was allowed to come back home, why would Ephraim not have to suffer similar refinement in the fire?

The Apostle Shaul tells us that there is no partiality with Elohim. That being the case, why would YHWH not treat the Two Houses equally?

> **Romim (Romans) 2:10-11**
> **10 but glory, honor, and peace to everyone who works what is good, to the Jew first and also to the Greek.**
> **11 For there is no partiality with Elohim.**

In fact, does not YHWH specifically *tell* us that Ephraim will suffer refinement in the fire? And does not Jeremiah come right out and *tell* us that YHWH will bring tribulation on Ephraim (to cleanse her of her iniquities), just prior to bringing her home?

> *Yirmeyahu (Jeremiah) 30:11*
> *11 "'For I am with you,' says YHWH, 'to save you. Though I make a complete end of all nations where I have scattered you, yet I will not make a complete end of you. But I will correct you in justice, and will not let you go altogether unpunished.'"*

Jeremiah then tell us that even though Ephraim seeks after her many lovers (of Sunday worship, Easter, Christmas, etcetera), all of these will abandon her. YHWH tells us He will cure Ephraim of her wayward desires by smiting her with "the wound of an enemy."

> *Yirmeyahu (Jeremiah) 30:12-14*
> *12 "For thus says YHWH:*
> *'Your affliction is incurable, your wound is severe.*
> *13 There is no one to plead your cause, that you may be bound up. You have no healing medicines.*
> *14 All your lovers have forgotten you. They do not seek you; for I have wounded you with the wound of an enemy, with the chastisement of a cruel one, for the multitude of your iniquities, because your sins have increased.*

YHWH will break Ephraim's desire for her lovers (i.e., her iniquities) by wounding her with a great and terrible wound (i.e., a tribulation). As we have already seen, Genesis 49:22-24 tells us that this will be an attack on mainland America by the Islamic people.

Jeremiah then tells us that when this attack comes, America's Christians will wail and cry incredulously at the punishment YHWH has brought upon them, not understanding that it was her own choices that forced YHWH to do this to her (to turn her back to Him).

> **Yirmeyahu (Jeremiah) 30:15**
> **15 Why do you cry about your affliction?**
> **Your sorrow is incurable. Because of the multitude of your iniquities, because your sins have increased, I have done these things to you.**

Poor Ephraim! She just does not seem to get it. It was a shock to Ephraim in the 9-1-1 Tragedy to realize that even though she loves all the other people of the world (perhaps even more than she loves YHWH), the other people of the world do not love her in return (and never will). Can she understand that YHWH had to allow the 9-1-1 Tragedy to happen to her, to wake her up from her delirious drunken cavorting with her many lovers, and to get her to return her attentions to Him?

Although it will be very hard on Ephraim to suffer this great wound from the Muslims, it is precisely because of YHWH's great love for Ephraim that He needs to allow her to be wounded. Only after she has been wounded will YHWH have her full attention; and then He can bring her out of Babylon.

But what does it mean, YHWH will bring Ephraim 'out of Babylon?' If the material world is a reflection of the spiritual world, then what exactly is involved in the Ephraimites 'coming out of Babylon?'

As we saw in the last two chapters, things in the material world are a *shadow* of the spiritual world. The Babylon we see, then, is a manifestation of a spirit called Babylon, and one way that the Spirit named Babylon manifests herself is *as a place*.

> **B'reisheet (Genesis) 11:4**
> **4 And they said, Come, let us build us a city, and a tower, whose top (may reach) unto heaven, and let us make us a name, lest we be scattered abroad upon the face of the whole earth.**

If YHWH's land is a *place* where YHWH's values are supposed to prevail, then Babylon is just the opposite. Babylon is a place where YHWH's anointed leadership is not allowed to rule. It is a place where material goods are valued over the good spiritual things of YHWH. Babylon is a place where spiritual and material values (as well as the languages) are confused.

The historical Babylon lies in modern day Iraq, some 56 miles south of Baghdad. Although the historical Babylon had lain in ruins, before he was ousted by U.S. military forces, Saddam Hussein spent untold millions of dollars rebuilding the ancient city upon its original foundations. He also minted coins with his image on them, and had them emblazoned with the words, "Nebuchadnezzar II." By this, he meant to indicate that modern-day Iraq would conquer Israel militarily (as the Babylon of old had done).

In addition to manifesting itself as a place, the Spirit called Babylon also manifests herself as an attitude (or, literally, as a 'spirit'). And in addition to manifesting herself as a place and a spirit, Babylon also manifests herself as an *organization*.

Organizations are made up of people who share a common belief, and a common spirit. As we explained earlier, the Christian Church is '*Mystery* Babylon.'

> ***Gilyana (Revelation) 17:3-5***
> ***3 And he carried me away in the Spirit into a wilderness: and I saw a woman sitting upon a scarlet-colored beast, full of names of blasphemy, having seven heads and ten horns.***
> ***4 And the woman was arrayed in purple and scarlet, and decked with gold and precious stone and pearls, having in her hand a golden cup full of abominations, even the unclean things of her fornication,***
> ***5 and upon her forehead a name written, MYSTERY: BABYLON THE GREAT, THE MOTHER OF THE HARLOTS AND OF THE ABOMINATIONS OF THE EARTH.***

Mystery Babylon is a means of *appearing* to become a Hebrew, while actually staying in Babylon. It is a means of *seeming* to 'cross over' (from a focus on the material world to a focus on the things of YHWH), while continuing to disobey His commandments. It is as subtle and as simple as worshipping in the wrong names, and on the wrong days. It is not the Spirit of Truth that motivates this type of behavior.

In *Nazarene Israel*, we explained that the Church has been used to do a tremendous amount of good over the centuries. However, this does not alter the fact that since the Church considers itself to be the *replacement* of YHWH's people Israel, the Church is not His people. (And so, whose people are they?)

Four verses later, Revelation 17:9 tells us that the woman (with the name '*Mystery*' Babylon written on her forehead) sits upon seven hills (or seven mountains). These are the Seven Hills of Rome.

> ***Gilyana (Revelation) 17:9***
> ***9 Here is the mind having wisdom. The seven heads are seven mountains, upon which the woman sits.***

Ultimately, Revelation gives us enough clues to identify the woman who rides the Beast (or the Roman System) as the Church (which is centered in Rome). (For more information, please see the *Nazarene Israel* study.)

So if Babylon is an *attitude* which values the things of the world more than the things of YHWH, then is there a *place* where this attitude (or this *spirit*) is more prevalent? Is there a land where material goods are valued more than the things of YHWH? Most countries fit this description, but is there one that stands out, head and shoulders above the rest?

That is, if the physical world is a reflection of the spiritual world, is there a physical place in the material world where *self-exaltation* is considered to be almost a virtue? And what would it tell us about the spirit of that place, that *self-exaltation* and *individuality* (rather than humility and community) would be considered virtues?

Jeremiah 50-51 gives us a comprehensive description of a physical land where self-exaltation and individuality take precedence over humility, family and community. In Jeremiah, that land is called Babylon (also called Chaldea).

Jeremiah 50-51 prophesies numerous catastrophes that will take place against this 'Babylon' in the end times. However, for some reason, the descriptions of this Babylon do not seem to fit the historical Babylon. Rather, they seem more like a description of America.

The Babylon of Jeremiah 50 will be a land of many idols and graven images, just as we find (both materially and spiritually) over much of America today. Jeremiah tells us that when Babylon is invaded from the north, these idols will be broken in pieces. As we will see below, such an invasion could easily come from either Russia or China, if they were to send missiles and/or troop aircraft over the North Pole.

> *Yirmeyahu (Jeremiah) 50:1-3*
> *1 The word that YHWH spoke against Babylon and against the land of the Chaldeans by Yirmeyahu the prophet.*
> *2 "Declare among the nations, proclaim, and set up a standard; proclaim — do not conceal it! Say, 'Babylon is taken, Bel is shamed! Merodach is broken in pieces! Her idols are humiliated, her images are broken in pieces.'*
> *3 For out of the north a nation comes up against her, which shall make her land desolate, and no one shall dwell therein. They shall move, they shall depart, both man and beast.*

Jeremiah then tells us that in the days when Babylon is destroyed, both Ephraimites and Jews will come back to the Land of Israel, weeping. This is interesting, in that more Jews presently live in America than live in the Land of Israel.

> **Yirmeyahu (Jeremiah) 50:4-5**
> **4 "In those days and in that time," says YHWH, "The children of Israel shall come, they and the children of Judah together. With continual weeping they shall come, and seek YHWH their Elohim.**
> **5 They shall ask the way to Zion, with their faces toward it, saying, 'Come and let us join ourselves to YHWH in a perpetual covenant that will not be forgotten.'"**

Although the exact timeline is not known, we showed earlier in '*The Millennial Land*' how the Muslim people will attack both Israel and America in coming years, and how YHWH will give victory both to Israel and to America. That is probably not the war being described here, as this attack comes from the north.

The exact sequence of events is not known. However, since the Islamic attacks on America will likely be used to expand the Land of Israel (see, '*The Millennial Land*,' above) and since there is likely more than one wave of immigration to the Millennial Land, one scenario that makes sense would be if the Islamic attacks came first on America, and one wave of immigration took place at that time, whereas a second wave of immigration took place during the time frame that Jeremiah describes here, when America is attacked from the north.

Although we do not know the time frame, by putting the pieces of the prophetic jigsaw puzzle together, we find a scenario that looks something like this:

1. Ephraim starts to form as a Stick.
2. The Islamic nations attack Israel and America.
3. America and Israel emerge victorious (all thanks and praise to YHWH).
4. The Land of Israel is greatly expanded, and a first wave of Ephraimite immigration returns to the Land.
5. After the first wave of immigration has left, America suffers a massive attack from the north (as per Jeremiah 50:3, above).
6. Another wave of immigration takes place.

If this sequence is correct, it might parallel the two-part immigration sequence that took place during Judah's restoration to the Land:

1. The Zionist Movement began (in 1896);
2. The Balfour Declaration (in 1917) allowed some Jews to immigrate (although most Jews stayed out in the Exile); and then
3. The Great Holocaust (in the early 1940's) took one-third of world Jewry as a 'burnt offering;' and then
4. The Nation of Israel was declared (in 1948), followed by large-scale immigration.

If we look closely, we should be able to see parallels between these lists. First there is a call for restoration to the Land, followed by restricted immigration, which is then followed by massive punishment on those who did not return, followed by large-scale immigration.

1. Agitation for restoration to the Land;
2. Limited immigration into the Land;
3. Punishment upon the rest of those who did not immigrate; followed by
4. Large-scale immigration.

While believers on Yeshua are not presently allowed to immigrate to the Land of Israel, Zechariah tells us that YHWH will change Judah's mind for him, by pouring out His Spirit of Grace and Supplication upon him.

> ***Zechariah 12:10***
> ***10 And I will pour upon the House of David and upon the inhabitants of Jerusalem the Spirit of Grace and of Supplication; and they shall look unto Me whom they have pierced; and they shall mourn for Him, as one mourns for his only son, and shall be in bitterness for Him, as one that is in bitterness for (the loss of) his first-born.***

Judah will supplicate (humbly and sincerely appeal to YHWH), perhaps out of desperation, and YHWH will respond by showing Judah that Yeshua is the Messiah.

Exactly at what point in this sequence YHWH will pour out His Spirit upon Judah, we do not know. However, it seems logical that it must happen prior to the first wave of Ephraimite immigration, because before anyone from Ephraim can relocate to the Land, Judah will have to be open to the idea of Ephraimite settlement. One can easily imagine that this will be a slow process that will culminate in watershed event.

This scenario also accords well with the world we see around us in the daily news. At the time of this writing (6007/2007CE), one can already see how Elohim is working upon Judah's hearts (by His Spirit). Israeli news agencies are beginning to make a big story out of the religious persecution that Messianic Jews face daily in the Land of Israel.

One of the interesting things about the spiritual realm is that for each and every spiritual action, there is an equal but opposite reaction. When one does good, and is persecuted for it, there is a backlash effect upon those who perform the persecution. The apostles were all persecuted (as were the early Christians), and the backlash was that belief on Yeshua became accepted in the ancient Roman world (and those suffering the persecution earned an incomparable eternal reward).

In South Africa in the early 1900's, an attorney named Mohandas Gandhi petitioned for civil rights for Indians living in South Africa. While he suffered many abuses for his civil rights actions, his non-violent response appealed to the Christian sensibilities of the English. Few people know that, although Gandhi was a Hindu, he was inspired by the teachings of Yeshua, and he based his principles of 'non-violence' on the Renewed Covenant. He was ultimately successful not only in bringing some civil liberties to South Africa, but also in winning Indian independence from Great Britain.

In America in the 1960's, a Christian pastor named Martin Luther King, Junior, won civil liberties for African Americans, by following a program of peaceful civil demonstrations that was based on Gandhi's campaign. Although King was later assassinated, his non-violent protests and suffering in the face of persecution won civil liberties for America's racial minorities.

The only reason we mention Gandhi and King is to point out that spiritual principles are not confined to the Hebrew faith: they work for Hindus and Christians also, because YHWH rewards good, no matter who does it. However, if peacefully suffering injustice works for non-Hebraic peoples such as Hindus and Christians, then how much more will YHWH bless those who are practicing the faith once delivered to the saints?

In the Land of Israel today, a Jew can make Aliyah (i.e., immigrate) no matter what religion he keeps, so long as he does not believe on Yeshua. Jews can make Aliyah if their religious persuasion is Orthodox, Conservative, Reform, Reconstructionist, Hasidic, Karaite, Buddhist, Hindu, Taoist, New Age, agnostic, or even Wiccan or Satanist. A Jew can practice any religion at all, except the belief on Yeshua. However, that is all changing now, as Judah is publicly asking themselves why they are so fiercely opposed to Messianic Jews, considering the fact that the Messianic Jews are loyal, circumcise their children, keep the correct days of worship, speak Hebrew, and serve in the Israeli Defense Forces (IDF).

Due to YHWH's working on Judah's heart, it is only a matter of time before the masses of Judah decide to outlaw the persecution of Messianic Jews, and then ultimately accept Yeshua (re: Zechariah 12:10, above). Once that happens, it will be a simple step for Judah to understand and embrace the Two House Theory, since this is what Yeshua taught. Once open to the Two House Theory, they will then be open to the idea of Ephraimite immigration.

Once Judah understands the Two House Theory and is open to the idea of Ephraimite immigration, it will be time to relocate to Israel, in order to avoid the coming destruction upon America.

Jeremiah tells us that an assembly of great nations 'from the north country' (i.e., coming over the North Pole) will destroy Babylon (or Chaldea). At that time, America will be plundered.

> **Yirmeyahu (Jeremiah) 50:8-10**
> **8 "Move from the midst of Babylon! Go out of the land of the Chaldeans, and be like the rams before the flocks.**
> **9 For behold, I will raise and cause to come up against Babylon an assembly of great nations from the north country, and they shall array themselves against her. From there she shall be captured. Their arrows shall be like those of an expert warrior: none shall return in vain.**
> **10 And Chaldea shall become plunder; all who plunder her shall be satisfied," says YHWH.**

In this passage, YHWH is fairly clear that His people will need to come out of a specific land. And, as we will see, the only land that meets all of the necessary criteria is America.

Many scholars consider these 'great nations from the north country' to be Russia, China and their allies. Not surprisingly, the traditional airborne-flight route for both atomic missiles and troop aircraft is up and over the North Pole, making Russia and China the "lands of the north." Then, verse 10 tells us:

> **10 And Chaldea shall become plunder; all who plunder her shall be satisfied," says YHWH.**

If the 'land of Chaldea' that will be plundered were Iraq, then how would all who plunder her become satisfied? Iraq has some oil wealth, but Iraq is far from a rich nation. However, in contrast, if the land that shall be plundered is America, it is easy to see how these other nations would become "satisfied."

Jeremiah then describes a land in which the people became rich by gladly destroying His heritage. What is this, but Ephraim's embracing of secular materialism?

> **Yirmeyahu (Jeremiah) 50:11-13**
> **11 "Because you were glad, because you rejoiced, you destroyers of My heritage, because you have grown fat like a heifer threshing grain, and you bellow like bulls,**
> **12 Your mother shall be deeply ashamed;**
> **She who bore you shall be ashamed. Behold, the last of the nations of the nations shall be a wilderness, a dry land and a desert.**
> **13 Because of the wrath of YHWH she shall not be inhabited, but she shall be wholly desolate. Everyone who goes by Babylon shall be horrified and hiss at all her plagues.**

One can see how America would be reckoned as the 'last of the nations.' Moreover, if America were to be attacked by Chinese and Russian nuclear weapons, it would make sense that the land would become wholly desolate. All of this would be the punishment on America for abandoning her heritage, and allowing her greedy heart to become lifted up.

> *Yirmeyahu (Jeremiah) 50:23-24*
> *23 How the hammer of the whole earth has been cut apart and broken! How Babylon has become a desolation among the nations! I have laid a snare for you;*
> *24 You have indeed been trapped, O Babylon, and you were not aware! You have been found and also caught, because you have contended against YHWH.*

The moniker "hammer of the whole earth" is consistent with America's role as the 'World's Policeman.' Then YHWH tells us that because of Babylon's pride against Him, YHWH will summon the archers against her, and will light a fire in her cities (perhaps from nuclear warheads).

> *Yirmeyahu (Jeremiah) 50:29-32*
> *29 "Call together the archers against Babylon. All you who bend the bow, encamp against it all around. Let none of them escape. Repay her according to her work! According to all she has done, do to her, for she has been proud against YHWH, against the Set-apart One of Israel.*
> *30 Therefore her young men shall fall in the streets, and all her men of war shall be cut off in that day," says YHWH.*
> *31 "Behold, I am against you, O most haughty one!" says YHWH Elohim of hosts; "For your day has come, the time that I will punish you.*

> *32 The most proud shall stumble and fall, and no one will raise him up. I will kindle a fire in his cities, and it will devour all around him."*

While the timing of these events is not clear, YHWH verifies that Babylon is a home to *some* of His people, which He identifies as the oppressed captives of both houses of Israel (both Ephraim and Judah). YHWH says He will rescue His people, while causing disquiet to the rest of the inhabitants of Babylon.

> *Yirmeyahu (Jeremiah) 50:33-34*
> *33 Thus says YHWH of hosts: "The children of Israel were oppressed, along with the children of Judah. All who took them captive have held them fast; they have refused to let them go.*
> *34 Their Redeemer is strong; YHWH of hosts is His name. He will thoroughly plead their case, that He may give rest to the land, but disquiet the inhabitants of Babylon.*

Then YHWH tells us that there will be a sword upon all of Babylon's horses, and upon her chariots, and upon all of the 'mixed peoples' who are in her midst.

> *Yirmeyahu (Jeremiah) 50:37-38*
> *37 A sword is against their horses, against their chariots, and against all the mixed peoples who are in her midst, and they will become like women. A sword is against her treasures, and they will be robbed.*

38 A drought is against her waters, and they will be dried up, for it is the land of carved images, and they are insane with their idols.

The term, 'mixed peoples' applies much less to Iraq than it applies to America. However, we should note here that YHWH does not concern Himself so much with genetics, as He does with religious beliefs. As we explained in *Nazarene Israel*, the Scriptural definition of a 'nation' has far more to do with what religious beliefs one practices, than it has to do with genetics.

Further, what is this reference to a land of 'mixed peoples' that are insane with their idols, but America? The amount of satanic imagery in America is staggering. Satan's pyramid and the All-Seeing-Eye adorn the back of the U.S. dollar bill. In parks and in universities all across the nation, Greek, Roman, Babylonian and other temples are recreated to scale.

The Pyramid Arena in Memphis (Tennessee) has even been designed to appear capless, so as to recreate Satan's pyramid (as it appears on the back of the U.S. dollar bill). YHWH tells us that for lifting herself up against Him in this way, the land where the 'daughter of Babylon' dwells shall be deserted, and shall be uninhabited forevermore. That does not speak of Iraq.

Yirmeyahu (Jeremiah) 50:39-40
39 "Therefore the wild desert beasts shall dwell there with the jackals, and the ostriches shall dwell in it. It shall be inhabited no more forever, nor shall it be dwelt in from generation to generation.

> **40 As Elohim overthrew Sodom and Gomorrah and their neighbors," says YHWH, "So no one shall reside there, nor son of man dwell in it.**

The historical Babylon was never overthrown as Sodom and Gomorrah. However, if Russia and China (and perhaps also their allies, including Japan) were to attack the United States with nuclear weapons, the land could become such that no one would reside in the land of the daughter of Babylon any longer.

> **Yirmeyahu (Jeremiah) 50:41-42**
> **41 "Behold, a people shall come from the north, and a great nation and many kings shall be raised up from the ends of the earth.**
> **42 They shall hold the bow and the lance; they are cruel and shall not show mercy. Their voice shall roar like the sea. They shall ride on horses, set in array, like a man for the battle, against you, O daughter of Babylon.**

One of the things that YHWH likes to do is to bring things to pass that seem impossible. This helps to build people's faith in His Word. While America may seem strong at the moment, YHWH says that He will bring foreign armies against the daughter of Babylon, and destroy her land utterly, so that mankind will never inhabit it again.

While we must fear and obey Elohim, we must also guard against panic. Many people are looking to flee America right now, based upon this verse, and others:

> *Yirmeyahu (Jeremiah) 51:6*
> *6 Flee from the midst of Babylon, and every one save his life! Do not be cut off in her iniquity, for this is the time of YHWH's vengeance!*
> *He shall recompense her.*

However, the time to flee America is probably not now. As we explained earlier in *'The Millennial Land,'* America and Israel are prophesied to fight against the Muslim people, and emerge victorious (all thanks and praise to YHWH). That cannot happen if America is already destroyed.

As we explained in *'The Millennial Land,'* the Land of Israel will be greatly expanded in the aftermath of the war with the Muslim nations. The first thing that any nation needs when it annexes new lands is settlers, and if the Ephraimites will continue to build the Stick of Ephraim, the Ephraimites could be ready.

As we saw in *'The Millennial Land,'* the 'mixed peoples' of Ephraim are prophesied to settle in the Gaza.

> *Zechariah 9:6*
> *6 "A mixed race shall settle in Ashdod (in Gaza), and I will cut off the pride of the Philistines (the Palestinians).*

We are also told that in the aftermath of the military victory, Ephraim will rejoice like a mighty man, and that his children shall rejoice in YHWH. That is unlikely to happen if the Ephraimites' homeland (America) is destroyed immediately following (or even during) the military conquest of the Middle East.

Zechariah 10:7-10
7 Those of Ephraim shall be like a mighty man, and their heart shall rejoice as if with wine. Yes, their children shall see it and be glad; their heart shall rejoice in YHWH.
8 I will whistle for them and gather them, for I will redeem them; and they shall increase as they once increased.
9 "I will sow them among the peoples, And they shall remember Me in far countries; they shall live, together with their children, and they shall return.
10 I will also bring them back from the land of Egypt, and gather them from Assyria. I will bring them into the land of Gilead and Lebanon, until no more room is found for them.

In contrast to the language of Jeremiah 50-51, the language in these passages does not speak of the Ephraimites leaving in haste, or going by flight. Rather, it speaks of the Ephraimites returning home exultant, as victors following a large-scale regional Middle-East war. Bearing this in mind, then the sequence we are looking at would be:

1. Judah forms a stick (starting in 1897, with Theodore Herzl and *'Der Judenstadt'*).
2. A small wave of Jewish immigration after the Balfour Declaration (circa 1917).
3. A third of the Jewish people are killed in the Great Holocaust.
4. Israel is declared as a nation (1948).
5. A larger wave of Jewish immigration goes to the Land of Israel.

6. Ephraim begins to form a stick, two thousand years after Messiah's birth (1996 or 2000 CE, depending upon whom one listens to).
7. Israel and America emerge victorious from war with the Islamic world (all thanks and praise to YHWH).
8. Ephraimite immigration possible.
9. Destruction of America (re: Jeremiah 50-51), coupled with a large wave of Ephraimite/Jewish immigration.

While the exact dates are not known, since YHWH does not play favorites, and since He is not a respecter of persons, it seems logical that He would use the same kind of refinement pattern for Ephraim, as He used with Judah.

if this sequence is correct, then once Judah is saved, and Aliyah is made available to the Ephraimite people, it would be exceedingly wise for all Ephraimites and Jews to take it (and *not* stay out in the Dispersion).

It is true that America is a very prosperous land.

> **Yirmeyahu (Jeremiah) 51:7**
> **7 Babylon was a golden cup in YHWH's hand that made all the earth drunk. The nations drank her wine; therefore the nations went mad.**

However, although America is a prosperous land in the material sense, America is a land of confused spiritual values. All the nations have drunk of the wine of America's materialistic, greedy, unrighteous conduct: that is why the nations went mad (i.e., materialistic).

The daughter of Babylon has been a tool in YHWH's hand. He has used her for His purposes. She will continue to be a tool in YHWH's hand until she has been used to help establish the Millennial Land of Israel (so that the Stick of Ephraim can go home), and then there will be no more use for her.

After the war against Islam is won, it will be high time to leave the daughter of Babylon. Although YHWH will protect the second wave of immigration (i.e., the Second Exodus, Jeremiah 50:33-34, above), wouldn't it be better to be part of the first wave of immigration, so that one does not have to survive the coming military onslaught against America?

> *Yirmeyahu (Jeremiah) 51:13*
> *13 O you who dwell on many waters, abundant in treasures, your end has come, the measure of your greedy gain.*

We know that this is a reference to America because Iraq is a landlocked country, and is not relatively great in treasures. In contrast, America dwells upon many waters: and no one rivals the excesses of greedy gain like capitalist America.

Isaiah also writes about the daughter of Babylon's destruction.

> *Yeshayahu (Isaiah) 47:1-7*
> *47:1 "Come down and sit in the dust, O virgin daughter of Babylon! Sit on the ground without a throne, daughter of the Chaldeans! For you shall no more be called tender and delicate.*

> 2 Take the millstones and grind meal. Remove your veil, take off the skirt, uncover the thigh, pass through the rivers.
> 3 Your nakedness shall be uncovered. Yes, your shame will be seen. I will take vengeance, and I will not arbitrate with a man."
> 4 As for our Redeemer, YHWH of hosts is His name, the Set-apart One of Israel.
> 5 "Sit in silence, and go into darkness, daughter of the Chaldeans! For you shall no longer be called the Lady of Kingdoms.
> 6 I was angry with My people; I have profaned My inheritance, and given them into your hand. You showed them no mercy. On the elderly you laid your yoke very heavily.
> 7 And you said, 'I shall be a lady forever,' so that you did not take these things to heart, nor remember the latter end of them.

As a whole, America does not fear YHWH. Instead, she believes she will be a lady 'forever' because of the strength of her own right hand.

We should also note that in verse 6, YHWH counts it as evil that the Babylonians do not take care of their elderly. The purpose of the third tithe is to take care of the sick, the poor, and the elderly. However, because the Church does not really think of itself as a family (but as a collection of families), the Church (i.e., *Mystery Babylon*) sees no requirement to take care of its own.

Isaiah describes the daughter of Babylon as a nation given to the pursuit of pleasures, which dwells securely (or which did dwell securely before 9-1-1). Then Isaiah talks about America's punishment for having exalted herself against YHWH (and for ignoring His Torah).

> *Yeshayahu (Isaiah) 47:8-11*
> *8 "Therefore hear this now, you who are given to pleasures, who dwell securely, who say in your heart, 'I am, and there is no one else besides me! I shall not sit as a widow, nor shall I know the loss of children!'*
> *9 But these two things shall come to you in a moment, in one day: the loss of children, and widowhood. They shall come upon you in their fullness because of the multitude of your sorceries, for the great abundance of your enchantments.*
> *10 "For you have trusted in your wickedness! You have said, 'No one sees me!' Your wisdom and your knowledge have warped you, and you have said in your heart, 'I am, and there is no one else besides me.'*
> *11 Therefore evil shall come upon you. You shall not know from where it arises, and trouble shall fall upon you. You will not be able to put it off. And desolation shall come upon you suddenly, which you shall not know.*

Who is given to pleasures more than America? And who says in her heart, "I reign forever?" Is there any nation that meets this criterion, but America?

> *Yeshayahu (Isaiah) 47:12-15*
> *12 "Stand now with your enchantments and the multitude of your sorceries in which you have labored from your youth. Perhaps you will be able to profit? Perhaps you will prevail?*
> *13 You are wearied in the multitude of your counsels! Let now the astrologers, the stargazers, and the monthly prognosticators stand up and save you from what shall come upon you.*
> *14 Behold, they shall be as stubble, the fire shall burn them. They shall not deliver themselves from the power of the flame. It shall not be a coal to be warmed by, nor a fire to sit before!*
> *15 Thus shall they be to you with whom you have labored, your merchants from your youth. They shall wander each one to his quarter. No one shall save you.*

As a democracy, America has a 'multitude of counsels' in her many political representatives. America will be increasingly wearied by this 'multitude of counsels' in the coming years.

Democracies hold that power and authority derive from the people (and not from Elohim). Because of this, democracies are inherently weak. America now has some thirteen million Muslims, and Islamic political representatives. Because her power and authority comes from the masses, America will not be able to withstand the growing Muslim threat in coming years.

One of the reasons Democracy is weak is because it is based on compromise between differing self interests. When the enemy is not a significant minority of the electorate, it does not cause division within the house. However, when an enemy forms a significant minority of the electorate, there can be no real resolve against it, because the enemy has the vote.

The Hebrew word for Babylon is 'Bavel' (בָּבֶל). The letter Bet (ב) is a picture of a house, and the letter Lamed (ל) is a picture of a goad, or a staff (which represents authority). The word picture for 'Bavel' is house-house-lamed (בבל), meaning that authority is split between two different houses (as of a legislature). This is a perfect picture of democracy, and Yeshua tells us that this kind of government cannot help but fall.

> **Mattai (Matthew) 12:25**
> **25 But Yeshua knew their thoughts, and said to them: "Every kingdom divided against itself is brought to desolation, and every city or house divided against itself will not stand."**

While it may be very difficult for westerners living in a democracy to understand, democracy is actually a very unscriptural form of government. What is supposed to happen is that when YHWH raises up someone (either to prophecy, to teach, to lead, or to judge), the people are supposed to recognize the anointing, and defer to it. However, this can only be done when people hear and obey His Voice.

America is also the 'daughter of Babylon' in that Babylon adopted religious plurality. It had a 'pantheon' of sorts, much like the New Age belief.

For example, Ishtar (also known as Easter) was a Babylonian goddess who was worshipped through temple cult prostitution. Ishtar welcomed religious pluralism by welcoming the elohim (g-ds) of the lands the Babylonian Empire had conquered into their pantheon.

Ishtar (Easter) was known as the goddess of freedom of religion. She was also called "The Mother of Immigrants," which calls to mind the Statue of Liberty.

The Statue of Liberty was designed by two French freemasons, and they reportedly patterned the statue after Ishtar. Ishtar was classically portrayed as wearing a crown, holding a torch in one hand and the Book of Hammurabi's Law in the other. This is an exact picture of the Statue of Liberty.

Ishtar was also known as Diana to the Greeks, and as Libertas to the Romans. It is from Libertas that the English word 'Liberty' comes, and thus, the Statue of Liberty is actually the graven image of Libertas (i.e., Ishtar, Ashtoreth, Astarte, or Diana). Does America's use of this symbol further YHWH's Kingdom here on earth? (And if not, then is it not just one more pagan symbol?)

There is also a New York suburb named Babylon. Prior to Saddam Hussein's rebuilding Babylon, the Babylon in New York was the only Babylon on earth. As one floats into Hudson Harbor, one can even see a banner that reads, "Welcome to Babylon."

If the material world is a reflection of the spiritual world, then what is the spiritual implication of a Statue of Ishtar, and what is the implication of a large banner in Hudson Harbor which reads, "Welcome to Babylon"?

American Christians behave as Babylonians do, each man placing the needs of his own family first. What we need to recognize is that YHWH wants Israel to behave like one big family. He wants Israel to be one big patriarchy that loves each other in spirit and in truth.

YHWH wants His family Israel to dwell in His land. However, before Israel can dwell in His land, first Israel must leave Babylon. This is not just a simple matter of selling our things and getting on the plane. First we must leave Babylon in our hearts (i.e., we must be cleansed of the Spirit of Babylon), and then YHWH will bring us back to His land, in the material realm.

In order to leave spiritual Babylon, we must stop thinking and behaving as Babylonians. We must stop putting ourselves and our own families first (but must put others first). This goes completely against the will of our flesh, but is that not the whole point of learning to walk in the Spirit?

The Abomination of Desolation

Many scholars believe that in 2007 CE, the earth is approximately 6007 years old. However, the Orthodox Jewish calendar tells us that in 2007 CE, the earth is really only 5767 years old. If we subtract 5767 from 6007, we see a difference of some 240 years between these two calendars.

```
  6007   Nazarene Israel calendar year (2007 CE)
 -5767   Orthodox Jewish calendar year
 = 240   Years of difference
```

The difference is approximately 240 or 241 years, since the calendars begin at different times of the year. Hut if there is 240 years difference between these two different calendars, then which one is right? And why would this question be important?

This question is important because if the year is 5767, then Yeshua was not the Messiah. However, if the year is 6007, Yeshua really was the Messiah. Further, an analysis of these things will show us what Scripture really teaches about the Abomination of Desolation.

As we explained before, the Apostle Kepha tells us that a day in prophecy is as a thousand earth years:

> **Kepha Bet (2nd Peter) 3:8**
> **8 But, beloved, do not forget this one thing: that (in prophecy) one day with YHWH is as a thousand years; and a thousand years is as one day.**

Let us apply this 'day for a thousand years' principle to the seven day Creation Week in Genesis.

> **B'reisheet (Genesis) 2:1-2**
> **1 Thus the heavens and the earth, and all the host of them, were finished.**
> **2 And on the seventh day Elohim ended His work which He had done, and He rested on the seventh day from all His work which He had done.**

If a day in prophecy represents a thousand earth years, then the seven days of the Creation Week are symbolic of a seven thousand year plan for the earth. At the end of these seven thousand years, Yeshua will come, and the earth will be burned up in fire (2nd Peter 3:10-12).

Interestingly, we can also see a picture of the Messiah in the Creation Week. Yeshua is symbolized by the spiritual light that Elohim created on the first day.

> **B'reisheet (Genesis) 1:3-5**
> **3 Then Elohim said, "Let there be light"; and there was light.**
> **4 And Elohim saw the light, that it was good; and Elohim divided the light from the darkness.**
> **5 Elohim called the light Day, and the darkness He called Night. So the evening and the morning were the first day.**

Since the sun was not created until the fourth day, the 'light' that Yeshua represents here is not visible light, but spiritual light.

Yochanan also tells us that Yeshua is the spiritual light of the world.

> **Yochanan (John) 1:1-5**
> **1 In the beginning was the Word, and the Word was with Elohim, and the Word was Elohim.**
> **2 He was in the beginning with Elohim.**
> **3 All things were made through Him, and without Him nothing was made that was made.**
> **4 In Him was life, and the life was the light of men.**
> **5 And the light shines in the darkness, and the darkness did not comprehend it.**

But in addition to being the spiritual light of the world, Yeshua is also symbolized by the sun that was made on the fourth day. Nazarenes, Christians and Orthodox Jews all agree that the sun is symbolic of the Messiah.

> **B'reisheet (Genesis) 1:14-19**
> **14 Then Elohim said, "Let there be lights in the firmament of the heavens to divide the day from the night; and let them be for signs and seasons, and for days and years;**
> **15 and let them be for lights in the firmament of the heavens to give light on the earth"; and it was so.**
> **16 Then Elohim made two great lights: the greater light to rule the day, and the lesser light to rule the night. He made the stars also.**

> **17 Elohim set them in the firmament of the heavens to give light on the earth,**
> **18 and to rule over the day and over the night, and to divide the light from the darkness. And Elohim saw that it was good.**
> **19 So the evening and the morning were the fourth day.**

Some Christians have suggested that since the sun is symbolic of the Messiah, it is OK to worship on the day of the sun ('Sunday'), and on the Roman solar calendar (the Christian calendar) in general. However, since Yeshua said He did not come to do away with the least part of the Torah (e.g. Matthew 5:17-19), it would be wrong to think that we can worship or rest on any other days than the ones which are specified in Scripture.

However, what we need to realize is that if:

1. the sun is symbolic of the Messiah, and if
2. the sun was created on the fourth day, and if
3. one day in prophecy is equal to a thousand earth years,
4. then we should expect that the Messiah would have been born at the 4000 year mark (i.e., at or near the end of the fourth prophetic day).

Nazarenes, Christians and Orthodox Jews all agree that the Messiah was to be born at the four thousand year mark, in fulfillment of the creation of the sun at Genesis 1:14-19 (above). And, if we add up the ages of certain people in the Tanach (the 'Old' Covenant), and add up the reigns of the kings, we get an age of the earth that is very close to 6007.

To read the full study and verify the details of the chronology, please see 'About the Missing 240 years,' at www.nazareneisrael.org, on the Free Studies page. What the article shows is that the exact number cannot be arrived at, because the ages of persons recorded in the Tanach are rounded down to the whole year. For example, Adam is said to have fathered Seth when he was 130 years old.

> **B'reisheet (Genesis) 5:3**
> **3 And Adam lived one hundred and thirty years, and begot a son in his own likeness, after his image, and named him Seth.**

It is highly unlikely that Adam was exactly one hundred and thirty years of age, to the day. That is, it is very unlikely that he was 130 years, 0 months and 0 days old when Seth was born. Rather, he was probably somewhere in between 130 and 131 years of age. In correcting for this kind of error, we come up with a total age of the earth somewhere within 2.5 to 6.5 years of 6,007 years, which is highly statistically significant. The age of the earth according to the Tanach is within 0.1625% of the 6,007 year total, which is very accurate, and this suggests that Yeshua really was the Messiah.

In contrast, if we take the present year of the Jewish calendar in 2007 CE (5767) and subtract the number of years from Yeshua's birth (2007), the Jewish calendar tells us that Yeshua was not born in the year 4,000, but in the year 3760.

5767	Jewish Calendar year
-2007	Minus the Christian year
=3760	Year of Yeshua's birth on the Jewish calendar

In the Jewish mind, that Yeshua was allegedly born in the year 3,760 completely disqualifies Him as being the Messiah. A birth age for Yeshua of 3,760 is 240 years off of the expected 4,000 year total. 240 years is too great of a discrepancy to be a fulfillment of the 4,000 year birth age stipulated by Genesis 1:14-19.

However, when we start to dig into this question of the exact age of the earth, what we find is that the Jewish calendar is inaccurate. Rather than calculating the age of the earth by adding up the dates in the Tanach (as we do in the study, 'About the Missing 240 years), the Jewish calendar is determined by a separate tradition.

What is this separate tradition? It is an official rabbinic chronology found in a book called the 'Seder Olam' ('The Order of Eternity').

Scholars disagree as to exactly when the Seder Olam was written. Some date it to about 169 CE, while yet others date it to around 240 CE. In either case, it was written more than a hundred years after Yeshua's death, burial and resurrection.

Most scholars agree that the Seder Olam is not accurate, and there is also general agreement that a few parts of it have been re-written many times, in an attempt to correct some fundamental errors in the text. However, the text even as it stands today is not correct.

Most believing scholars also agree that the Seder Olam was written in order to justify subtracting 240 years from the rabbinical calendar, so as to prove that Yeshua was not really born in the year 4,000 (and hence, that He was not really the Messiah). But how could the Jews decide to subtract 240 years from their calendar? And why did they do it?

Since they also study prophecy, the rabbis expected the Messiah to be born in the Hebrew year 4000 (0 CE). However, the Jewish conception of a 'messiah' is that of a great military leader who vanquishes Israel's enemies, and brings the people back to the Torah. Since Yeshua did not throw off the Roman army (but was killed), and since many people misunderstood His teachings (that the rabbinical customs in the Talmud were not part of the Torah), the rabbis did not see how Yeshua was the prophesied messiah. For this reason, they continued to look for a great military leader.

In the original Hebrew calendar year 4133 (133 CE), about a hundred years after Yeshua's ministry, there was a man by the name of Simon ben Cosiba. Simon ben Cosiba's was a great military leader, and so his name was later changed to Simon Bar Kochba (Simon, son of the star) due to the rabbinical belief that he was the messianic fulfillment of Numbers 24:17.

> **Bemidbar (Numbers) 24:17**
> **17 "I see Him, but not now;**
> **I behold Him, but not near;**
> **A Star shall come out of Jacob;**
> **A Scepter shall rise out of Israel,**
> **And batter the brow of Moab,**
> **And destroy all the sons of tumult.**

The Jews had been suffering under Roman occupation even in Yeshua's day, but when the Romans outlawed physical circumcision and forbade the Jews to come to Jerusalem more than one day a year, the Jews rose up in violent protest. Whereas the Jews had never before been successful at throwing off the Roman yoke, Simon ben Cosiba unified the Jewish forces, and brought them together as one army.

Simon ben Cosiba won several key decisive military battles against the Romans. So powerful was the Jewish revolt, and so great were the Roman losses that the Romans committed twelve Roman legions against the Jews (which was something like a third to a half of the Roman military at that time). Even with half of their military committed to the fighting, the Romans were still badly outnumbered, and they took heavy losses. They did not dare to fight on the open battleground, but took to a 'scorched earth' policy that over time eroded the Jewish ability to fight.

Because of his military successes against the Romans, the leading rabbi of the day (Rabbi Akiva) declared that Simon Ben Cosiba was the messiah. However, since the rabbis were aware that the Messiah had to be born in the year 4,000 (0 CE), the rabbis decreed that 240 years had to be subtracted from the Jewish calendar. This was done in order to make it look like Shimon Ben Cosiba was fulfilling some of the prophecies over the Messiah in Daniel 9:24-27. At the time of the decree, the year changed from 4133 to 3893 overnight.

Modern Jewish scholarship acknowledges that the Seder Olam is inaccurate. Under the heading 'Seder Olam,' the Encyclopedia Judaica tells us that there is some "significant confusion" in the author's calculations, including several places where the amount of time attributed to the 'Persian Period' was 'compressed' from ten kingships, to just four.

Although Yose b. Halafta was probably not the author of the Seder Olam (in that he is quoted by the author, and is even derided by the author for making incorrect statements about the chronology), it is nonetheless instructive that modern Jewish scholarship admits that the Seder Olam's chronology was changed.

> *"Yose b. Halafta, the presumed author of Seder Olam Rabbah, probably had access to old traditions that also underlay the chronological computations of the Jewish Hellenistic chronographer Demetrius (third century B.C.E.). The most significant confusion in Yose´s calculation is the compression of the Persian period, from the rebuilding of the Temple by Zerubbabel in 516 B.C.E. to the conquest of Persia by Alexander (331 B.C.E.) to no more than 34 years."*

Just what exactly is the Encyclopedia Judaica saying?

The 'Persian Period' lasted approximately 185 years, and spanned ten kingships. It started in 516 BCE, and lasted until the conquest of Judea by Alexander the Great in 331 BCE. This equates to 185 years.

```
  516 BCE   Start of the Persian Period
 -331 BCE   End of the Persian Period
  =185      Duration of the Persian Period
```

In contrast, the Seder Olam tells us that the Persian Period lasted only 34 years, which is 151 years short.

```
  185   Duration of the Persian Period
  -34   Seder Olam's Persian Period
 =151   Discrepancy over the Persian Period
```

This is just one example of the kinds of 'compressions' and 'inaccuracies' found in the Seder Olam.

The author of the Seder Olam 'compressed' 151 years from the Persian Period, and even more time from other periods, for a total of 240 years of 'compression.' As a result of this, it made it look like Simon Ben Cosba (Simon Bar Kochba) fit the prophecies over the coming of the Messiah much better than Yeshua did.

Simon Bar Kochba was ultimately defeated by the Romans, and killed. Ironically, even though he was proven to be a false messiah, the rabbis still refuse to correct the 240 year subtraction.

The year in 2007 CE, however, is not 5767, but 6007. One additional advantage of knowing the correct year is that we can understand what Scripture really teaches us about the Abomination of Desolation.

In addition to the 'thousand years for a day' rule, we are also told that a day in prophecy can sometimes symbolize *one* earth year:

> ***Yehezqel (Ezekiel) 4:4-6***
> ***4 "Lie also on your left side, and lay the iniquity of the House of Israel upon it. According to the number of the days that you lie on it, you shall bear their iniquity.***
> ***5 For I have laid on you the years of their iniquity, according to the number of the days, three hundred and ninety days; so you shall bear the iniquity of the House of Israel.***
> ***6 And when you have completed them, lie again on your right side; then you shall bear the iniquity of the House of Judah forty days. I have laid on you a day for each year."***

That one prophetic day sometimes symbolizes just *one* earth year also helps to give us just one more witness as to why Pre-Millennial Return Theory is wrong.

Classical Pre-Millennial Return Theory tells us that the Messiah Yeshua was supposed to return in the clouds in physical form in 2000 CE. According to the classical doctrine, that means that the anti-Messiah was also supposed to come to power three and one-half years before that (i.e., in 1996 CE), so that the earth could have three and one-half years of tribulation before Yeshua's triumphal return in the clouds.

According to classical Pre-Millennial Return Theory, the anti-Messiah was also supposed to build an "anti-Messiah's Temple" starting in 1996 CE. According to Pre-Millennial Return Theory, this "anti-Messiah's Temple" was supposed to have been the prophetic fulfillment of the Abomination of Desolation that is spoken of by the prophet Daniel.

> **Daniel 12:11**
> **11 "And from the time that the daily (sacrifice) is taken away, until the Abomination of Desolation is set up, there shall be one thousand two hundred and ninety (1,290) days.**

But did the anti-Messiah come to power in 1996 CE? And did he build an anti-Messiah Temple in Jerusalem in 1996?

No, he did not: and yet somewhat amazingly, many people still claim that the anti-Messiah will do that very soon. However, if they would stop for a moment, they would see that this is impossible. But why?

The Abomination of Desolation must have been set up long before 1996 CE. Why? Because the 'days' in Daniel 12:11 represent earth years, according to the pattern shown in Ezekiel.

> **Yehezqel (Ezekiel) 4:6b**
> **6b "I have laid on you a (prophetic) day for each year."**

When Daniel 12:11 tells us that there would be 1,290 *days* in between the time the daily sacrifice was taken away until the Abomination of Desolation was set up, what Daniel really meant was that there would be 1,290 earth *years* in between the time the daily sacrifice was taken away, until the Abomination of Desolation was set up.

Daniel 12:11	
11 "And from the time that the daily (sacrifice) is taken away, until the Abomination of Desolation is given, there shall be one thousand two hundred and ninety (1290) days.	(11) וּמֵעֵת הוּסַר הַתָּמִיד וְלָתֵת שִׁקּוּץ שֹׁמֵם ׀ יָמִים אֶלֶף מָאתַיִם וְתִשְׁעִים

If Yeshua was born in the year 4000, then in 1996 CE (when the anti-Messiah was allegedly supposed to come), the earth was already 5996 years old.

```
 4000   Age of the earth at Yeshua's birth (0 CE)
+1996   Years since Yeshua's birth in 1996 CE
=5996   Age of the Earth in 1996 CE
```

Since the earth will only last for 7,000 years, in 1996 CE there were only 1,004 more years until the earth would be destroyed.

```
  5996   Age of the earth in 1996 CE
 +1004   Earth years remaining in 1996 CE
 =7000   Age of the earth at its destruction
```

However, Daniel 12:11 requires 1,290 years in between the time the daily sacrifice is taken away, until the Abomination of Desolation is set up.

> **Daniel 12:11**
> **11 "And from the time that the daily (sacrifice) is taken away, until the Abomination of Desolation is set up, there shall be one thousand two hundred and ninety (1,290) days.**

For there to be 1,290 days in between the time the daily is taken away and the time the Abomination of Desolation is set up, the daily sacrifice could not have been taken away any later than 1710 CE (prior to the American Revolution).

```
  5710   Daily taken away no later than this (1710 CE)
 +1290   1290 years to the Abomination of Desolation
 =7000   Earth is destroyed
```

However, as we already saw, in 1996 CE there were only 1,004 earth years remaining. Therefore, had an anti-Messiah 'taken away the daily' at any time after 1710 CE, there would not have been enough time left to fulfill Daniel 12:11.

What we need to realize is that the establishment of the Abomination of Desolation cannot be a *future* event, because that would force the earth to go beyond the 7,000 years allotted to it in prophecy. Therefore, the 'taking away of the daily sacrifice' and the setting up of the Abomination of Desolation can only be *past* events.

There were actually three different Babylonian attacks on Jerusalem, but the one in which the daily sacrifice was taken away was in 597/596 BCE, under the reign of King Yehoiachin.

Second Kings 24:10-14 tells us that Nebuchadnezzar, the king of Babylon, captured Jerusalem in the eighth year of his reign. Secular history tells us that the eighth year of Nebuchadnezzar's reign was approximately 597/596 BCE. Verse 13 tells us that not only did Nebuchadnezzar's forces take away all of the priests, but they also took away all of the utensils used for serving in the Temple, which meant that the priesthood could no longer offer up the daily sacrifices (and therefore, the daily sacrifice was taken away).

> *Melachim Bet (2nd Kings) 24:10-14*
> *10 At that time the servants of Nebuchadnezzar king of Babylon came up against Jerusalem, and the city was besieged.*
> *11 And Nebuchadnezzar king of Babylon came against the city, as his servants were besieging it.*
> *12 Then Yehoiachin, king of Judah, his mother, his servants, his princes, and his officers went out to the king of Babylon; and the king of Babylon, in the eighth year of his reign, took him prisoner.*

> **13 And he carried out from there all the treasures of the House of YHWH and the treasures of the king's house, and he cut in pieces all the articles of gold which Solomon king of Israel had made in the Temple of YHWH, as YHWH had said.**
>
> **14 Also he carried into captivity all Jerusalem: all the captains and all the mighty men of valor, ten thousand captives, and all the craftsmen and smiths. None remained except the poorest people of the land.**

The daily sacrifices were 'taken away' in 597/596 BCE, when Jerusalem fell. Notice, then, that Daniel 12:11 (above) tells us that from the time the daily sacrifice was taken away (in 597/596 BCE), there would be 1,290 days (i.e., 1,290 years) until the Abomination of Desolation would be set up. Therefore, to discover when the Abomination of Desolation was set up, all we need to do is just to add 1,290 years to the date that Jerusalem fell (in 597/596 BCE).

```
  -597   Jerusalem fell to Nebuchadnezzar (597 BCE)
 +1290   Years to the Abomination of Desolation
  =693   Dome of the Rock completed (693/694 CE)
```

An inscription in the Dome of the Rock claims that construction was completed in 691/692, and most Muslim authorities have accepted this as the official completion date. However, other renowned Muslim historians such as Sibt b. Al-Jawzi have argued that this date was inscribed prematurely, and that the work was not totally completed until 693/694 CE.

The Dome of the Rock is the perfect fulfillment of the Abomination of Desolation. From a Hebraic standpoint, it completely defiles the Temple Mount, making it impossible to re-establish the correct worship until it is destroyed. In effect, then, the Dome of the Rock makes Israel's worship 'desolate.'

Then in Daniel 12:12, we read about a blessing that comes to those who wait until the 1,335 days (i.e., 1,335 years).

> **Daniel 12:12**
> **12 Blessed is he who waits, and comes to the one thousand three hundred and thirty-five (1,335) days.**

If we add 1,335 years to the date that the Dome of the Rock (i.e., the Abomination of Desolation) was actually completed, we come to approximately (+/-) 2028 CE.

```
  693   Dome of the Rock established (693/694 CE)
+1335   Years to wait for the blessing (+1,335 years)
=2028   'The blessing' will be bestowed (2028/29 CE)
```

2028/2029 is a date we already recognize as being highly significant in prophecy. Ezekiel was told to lie on his left side for 390 days; each day symbolizing a year that the House of Ephraim was to remain in exile:

> **Yehezqel (Ezekiel) 4:4-5**
> **4 "Lie also on your left side, and lay the iniquity of the House of Israel upon it. According to the number of the days that you lie on it, you shall bear their iniquity.**

> *5 For I have laid on you the years of their iniquity, according to the number of the days: three hundred and ninety days; so you shall bear the iniquity of the House of Israel (or Ephraim).*

Again the 'day for a year' rule holds, so that the House of Israel (Ephraim) would not stay in the Assyrian Dispersion for just 390 days, but 390 *years*.

However, there was also a catch. Leviticus 26 tells us that whenever we do not obey all of His commandments, then He will set His face against us, and punish us.

> *Vayiqra (Leviticus) 26:14-17*
> *14 "But if you do not obey Me, and do not observe all these commandments,*
> *15 and if you despise My statutes, or if your soul abhors My judgments, so that you do not perform all My commandments, but break My Covenant,*
> *16 I also will do this to you:*
> *17 I will set My face against you, and you shall be defeated by your enemies. Those who hate you shall reign over you, and you shall flee when no one pursues you.*

Then verse 18 tells us something special. It tells us that if we are not performing *all* of His commandments at the end of our time of punishment, then He multiplies our punishment times seven. This is not seven *more* times, but a *total* of seven times.

Leviticus 26:18 18 And after all this, if you do not obey Me, then I will punish you seven times, for your sins.	(18) וְאִם עַד אֵלֶּה לֹא תִשְׁמְעוּ לִי ׀ וְיָסַפְתִּי לְיַסְּרָה אֶתְכֶם שֶׁבַע עַל חַטֹּאתֵיכֶם

In *Nazarene Israel*, we spoke about how YHWH used the Assyrian Empire to take the northern ten tribes of Israel into the Assyrian Diaspora, in fulfillment of the punishments prophesied in Ezekiel 4:4-5 (above). It is easy to think of this attack against the northern House of Israel (Ephraim) as being one single event, but that would be overly simplistic.

While Satan has always been bent on the destruction of Israel, the king of Assyria (Tiglath Pileser III) was probably not so much consciously intent on punishing the House Israel for YHWH as he was upon expanding his own empire. Much like the Greeks and the Romans who came after him, Tiglath-Pileser III was probably just seizing and holding what he felt were important economic and strategic pieces of ground, in order to expand his empire.

The military history of the region is complex. However, secular history informs us that Tiglath-Pileser began his incursions into the Northern Kingdom of Israel in approximately 738 BCE, and that there was a series of successive campaigns over several years. However, historians also agree that the year 734 BCE was highly significant, in that it was the year that the Mediterranean coastal strip fell, including the city of Gaza and most of Philistia.

Whenever the Assyrians conquered a piece of land, their practice was to deport the inhabitants of that land, and then re-settle the ground with others from the Assyrian Empire. There were numerous incremental deportations, but if the Assyrians made a major landmark deportation in 734 BCE, then 390 years later would bring us to 344 BCE.

```
-734   Assyrian deportation of Gaza and coastal zone
+390   Years of punishment prophesied on Ephraim
-344   End of the prophesied punishment (344 BCE)
```

As we explain in *Nazarene Israel*, the problem was that when our forefathers went into captivity, they did not take the punishment to heart. They did not begin keeping the Torah. Rather, after they were re-settled they lost their identity as Israelites, and began to think of themselves not so much as Ephraimites, but as Assyrians. This was witnessed by the fact that they no longer kept the Torah, no longer spoke Hebrew, and no longer lived in the Land of Israel. Thus, they lost their identity as His people. This is very similar to how many families in America and the rest of the ex-British Empire used to be very religious and devout, but their children have fallen away from the faith.

Because our forefathers did not begin keeping all of His Commandments when the time of punishment ran out (in 344 BCE), our punishment was multiplied times seven (for a total of seven times). Thus, the total years of punishment grew from 390 years, to seven times 390 years, for a total of 2,730 years.

```
  390    Initial years of punishment in Ezekiel 4:4-5
   x 7   Multiplication times seven (Leviticus 26:18)
=2,730   Total years of the Ephraimite Dispersion
```

When we add 2,730 years to the time of the Assyrian deportations of Gaza and the strategic Mediterranean coastal area (in 734 BCE), we find that the new end of Ephraim's dispersion comes to approximately 1996 CE.

-734	Assyrian deportations of Gaza and coast
+2730	Total years of punishment
=1996	New end of the Ephraimite Dispersion

As we will see below, 1996 CE is a highly significant date, in that it marks the beginning (but not the completion) of the end of Ephraim's dispersion. That is, Ephraim's dispersion would 'begin to end' at that time.

Just as the Jews were carried into captivity in Babylon over a long period of time, and just as the Ephraimites were carried into the Dispersion over a period of many years, so too will the end of the Dispersion take place over a period of time (rather than all at once).

The Book of Hosea also witnesses to the end of Ephraim's dispersion beginning to take place in or around 1996, and ending in approximately 2029 CE. The Book of Hosea speaks primarily to the House of Ephraim. Therefore, speaking of the Ephraimites, Hosea prophesies:

> **Hosea 6:2**
> *2 After two days He will revive us. In the third day He will raise us up, that we may live in His sight.*

Let us remember once again that a day in prophecy can equal a thousand earth years.

> **Kepha Bet (2nd Peter) 3:8**
> *8 But, beloved, do not forget this one thing, that with YHWH, one day is as a thousand years, and a thousand years as one day.*

If a prophetic day can equal a thousand earth years, then the two prophetic 'days' of Hosea 6:2 are really two thousand years, and what Hosea is telling us is that the Ephraimites will be raised up after two thousand years. But the next question becomes, "Two thousand years *from when*?"

The word *Mashiach* (Messiah) means 'anointed one,' and in Hebraic thought, a *Mashiach* is a divinely appointed leader who brings the lost and scattered of Israel back to the Land of Israel, and to the eternal Torah. As we showed in *Nazarene Israel*, this is what Yeshua is doing for the Ephraimite people.

Scholarship generally disagrees as to the exact year of the Messiah's birth. However, whether Yeshua was born in 4 BCE, 1 BCE, or 1AD (i.e., the year 0) is not really important to us, as we are not attempting to set exact dates. However, since most scholars now favor the 4 BCE date, let us use that date for this particular computation.

Just as Tiglath Pileser's dispersions of the Ephraimites took place over many years, the Ephraimite movement also has no exact pinpoint 'start date.' However, numerous persons active in the Two House and Ephraimite Movements have reported that 1996 CE was a pivotal year in the Two House Movement, in that the numbers of people attending the festivals greatly increased, and that there was also a dramatic surge in interest in that year in general.

Two thousand years after Yeshua's birth in 4 BCE brings us to 1996 CE, which is the same year that the Ephraimite movement reportedly enjoyed a dramatic surge of interest.

```
 -4     Likely date of Messiah Yeshua's birth (4 BCE)
+2000   Two thousand years of Hosea 6:2
=1996   Year the Ephraimite Movement grew
```

The dates are not exact, which is why one needs 'eyes to see' what is actually happening. However, since the job of a *Messiah* is to bring back the lost and the scattered of Israel, and to bring them back to the Torah, it only makes sense that the year of the Messiah's birth would be highly significant with regards to the Ephraimite Movement.

Even if we use the year 0 (or some other year, such as 1 BCE), the numbers still work for our purposes here, because all we are trying to do is to show that some time in the general vicinity of 1996 to 2000 CE, there was a dramatic surge in interest in the Ephraimite and the Two House movements; and that this is directly related to the fact that the Messiah was born some two thousand years before.

But if the year of the Messiah's birth is significant with regards to the Ephraimite Movement, then what about the year of the Messiah's death and resurrection? One would think that the death, burial and resurrection of the Messiah would be even more significant with regards to the Ingathering of Israel than the Messiah's birth was. What is 'two days' after that?

Scripture tells us that the Messiah began His ministry when He was about 30 years of age.

Luqa (Luke) 3:23
23 Now Yeshua Himself began His ministry at about thirty years of age, being (as was supposed) the son of Yosef....

Most scholars also generally believe that the Messiah's ministry lasted for some three and one-half years, thus putting His age at His resurrection at about 33-34.

-4	Yeshua's birth (approximately 4 BCE)
+33	Yeshua's age at His death and resurrection
=29	Yeshua's resurrection (approximately +/- 29 CE)

Two thousand years from Yeshua's death, burial and resurrection in +/- 29 CE, then, give us a third witness to the (approximate) 2028/2029 CE date.

29	Approximate date of Yeshua's resurrection
+2000	Two thousand years of Hosea 6:2
=2029	Ephraim is 'raised up' ('resurrected')

We should emphasize that we are not setting a date for the Ingathering, nor are we even specifying an exact year. The dates and figures we are working with here are ancient, and inexact. While YHWH knows the day and the hour He will bring His people back home, we do not need to know the day or the hour. Like good brides, all we need to do is to know what prophecy says, and then begin preparing ourselves for the day and the hour that He should decide to bring us home. At our level, what we need to know is that we cannot go home until we assemble ourselves as the 'Stick of Ephraim,' in order to fulfill Ezekiel 37:15-17.

> *Yehezqel (Ezekiel) 37:16b-17*
> *16b Then take another stick and write on it, 'For Joseph, the Stick of Ephraim, and for all the House of Israel, his companions.'*
> *17 <u>Then</u> join them one to another for yourself into one stick, and they will become one in your hand.*

However, before we close this chapter, we should also point out that there will also be a second fulfillment of the Abomination of Desolation in the end times, just before Yeshua's triumphal return.

> *Mattai (Matthew) 24:15-27*
> *15 "Therefore when you see the Abomination of Desolation spoken of by Daniel the prophet, standing in the Set-apart Place" (whoever reads, let him understand),*
> *16 "then let those who are in Judea flee to the mountains.*
> *17 Let him who is on the housetop not go down to take anything out of his house.*
> *18 And let him who is in the field not go back to get his clothes.*
> *19 But woe to those who are pregnant and to those who are nursing babies in those days!*
> *20 And pray that your flight may not be in winter or on the Sabbath.*
> *21 For then there will be great tribulation, such as has not been since the beginning of the world until this time, no, nor ever shall be.*

> **22** And unless those days were shortened, no flesh would be saved; but for the elect's sake those days will be shortened.
> **23** "Then if anyone says to you, 'Look, here is the Messiah!' or 'There!' do not believe it.
> **24** For false messiahs and false prophets will rise and show great signs and wonders to deceive, if possible, even the elect.
> **25** See, I have told you beforehand.
> **26** "Therefore if they say to you, 'Look, He is in the desert!' do not go out; or 'Look, He is in the inner rooms!' do not believe it.
> **27** For as the lightning comes from the east and flashes to the west, so also will the coming of the Son of Man be.

As we mentioned before, YHWH sometimes inspires Scripture in riddles, in order to keep the meanings of certain books 'sealed up' until the end times.

In Matthew 24:15-17 (above) Yeshua is actually telling us that there will be a second Abomination of Desolation set up on the Temple Mount (the Set-apart Place). This second Abomination of Desolation will be set up during the Great Tribulation, which comes just prior to Yeshua's victorious return at the end of the Millennium. The reason we know this is that there was no reason for those in Jerusalem to have to flee to the mountains when the first Abomination of Desolation was set up in 693/694 CE. This need to flee will only take place when Jerusalem is overrun, during the Great Tribulation at the end of the Millennium.

At the end of the Millennium, Satan will be loosed from his prison, and he will go forth to marshal all of the armies of the world together against Israel in the War of Gog and Magog. In this war, Israel will be overrun, and the Great Tribulation will begin. Satan's Forces will once again take away all of the daily sacrifices, and an Abomination That Makes Desolate will again be set up on the Temple Mount.

> *Gilyana (Revelation) 20:7-9*
> *7 Now when the thousand years have expired, Satan will be released from his prison*
> *8 and will go out to deceive the nations which are in the four corners of the earth, Gog and Magog, to gather them together to battle, whose number is as the sand of the sea.*
> *9a They went up on the breadth of the earth and surrounded the camp of the saints and the beloved city (and overran it - - NBW).*
> *9b And (after a time) fire came down from Elohim out of heaven and devoured them.*

At the end of the Millennium, Satan will be loosed from his prison, and will go forth to marshal all of the armies of the world together against Israel, in the War of Gog and Magog. Israel will be overrun, and Jerusalem will be taken. The Great Tribulation will begin as Satan's forces will again take away the daily sacrifices, and an Abomination of Desolation will again established be on the Temple Mount. It is at this time that Yeshua will appear in the clouds, and catch His people up to be with Him, and fight against Satan's forces (and win).

Zechariah 14:1-5
14:1 Behold, the day of YHWH is coming, and your spoil will be divided in your midst.
2 For I will gather all the nations to battle against Jerusalem. The city shall be taken, the houses rifled, and the women ravished. Half of the city shall go into captivity, but the remnant of the people shall not be cut off from the city.
3 Then YHWH will go forth and fight against those nations, as He fights in the day of battle.
4 And in that day His feet will stand on the Mount of Olives, which faces Jerusalem on the east, and the Mount of Olives shall be split in two, from east to west, making a very large valley. Half of the mountain shall move toward the north, and half of it toward the south.
5 Then you shall flee through My mountain valley, for the mountain valley shall reach to Azal. Yes, you shall flee as you fled from the earthquake in the days of Uzziah king of Judah. Thus YHWH my Elohim will come, and all the saints with You.

As we read in Revelation 20:9b (above), fire will come down from heaven, and destroy Satan's forces. This will happen when Yeshua (who is also YHWH) calls down fire from YHWH in heaven (i.e., YHWH the Father) upon the armies of Gog and Magog, just as He called down fire at Sodom and Gomorrah.

> *B'reisheet (Genesis) 19:24-25*
> *24 Then YHWH rained brimstone and fire on Sodom and Gomorrah, from YHWH out of the heavens.*
> *25 So He overthrew those cities, all the plain, all the inhabitants of the cities, and what grew on the ground.*

In the Great Tribulation at the end of the Millennium, Yeshua comes to save His bride Israel from destruction at the hand of the armies of Gog and Magog, and then He will take all the wise virgins to the Wedding Feast that is right now being prepared at His Father's house.

May you be among those wise virgins.

In Yeshua's name,

Amein.

Building the Stick

In *Nazarene Israel*, we showed what the original faith of the apostles actually was. In *Joseph's Return*, we have seen how the Messiah does not return physically in the clouds at the start of the Millennium, but how He returns only at the Millennium's end, to save His bride Israel from destruction.

We have also seen how the Ephraimite people must organize themselves into a nation (or a 'stick'), before they can return back home to the Land of Israel. And lastly, we saw how destruction is prophesied to come on America, the Daughter of Babylon.

If America is prophesied to be destroyed, and if the Ephraimite people cannot return home until they form a reunited nation (or a 'stick'), then it would behoove all of us who would escape America's coming destruction, to reason together, and figure out how to build the Stick of Ephraim, so we can return back home to the Land of Israel, before destruction comes upon us.

In future works we will talk about the specifics of what it will take for Ephraim to build the Stick of Ephraim, so that YHWH may restore the Ephraimites to the Land of their inheritance.

May it be so, soon and in our day.

In Yeshua's name,

Amein.

"And behold, I am coming quickly, and My reward is with Me, to give to every one according to his work."

Revelation 22:12

Book Ordering Information:

All of our books and instructional materials are available either for free download on the Internet, or print on demand at cost through **www.amazon.com**.

May the Name of YHWH of Hosts be glorified and magnified among His people Israel, and may the faith once delivered to the saints be restored among all of His people, soon and in our day.

In Yeshua's name,

Amein.

Donations to Nazarene Israel:

YHWH promises to bless those who cheerfully give to His work (e.g., Exodus 25:2, Malachi 3:10). If you would like to receive your blessing for cheerfully giving back part of what your Creator gives you, we ask that you pray, and then do as He leads you.

Donations can be sent electronically through the website, at **www.nazareneisrael.org**, or you can send it through the post, to:

Nazarene Israel
PO Box 787
Anderson, CA 96007
USA

Please know that your donations will be carefully and fearfully handled for the furtherance of His Kingdom.

May the Name of YHWH be glorified: Shalom.

Write the vision
And make it plain on tablets;
That he who reads it runs.

Habakkuk 2:2

Made in the USA
Lexington, KY
24 April 2011